AYATULLAH IBRAHIM AMINI

Knowing God

First published by Ansariyan Publications 2011

Copyright © 2011 by Ayatullah Ibrahim Amini

All rights reserved. No part of this publication may be reproduced, stored or transmitted in any form or by any means, electronic, mechanical, photocopying, recording, scanning, or otherwise without written permission from the publisher. It is illegal to copy this book, post it to a website, or distribute it by any other means without permission.

First edition

Translation by Sayyid Athar Husayn S.H. Rizvi

Contents

Foreword	1
Preface	5
Materialistic and Religious World View; Effects and...	11
World in the View of Believers	11
End of Life	12
Creator of the Universe	13
Prophets	13
Who am I?	15
Where have I come from?	15
Where am I?	15
Where am I going?	15
Fruits of Belief in this Life	16
1. Hope	17
2. Optimism About The End Of Life	18
3. Recognition of Duty	20
4. Satisfaction	21
5. Patience and Determination	23
But What Is The Condition Of The Disbeliever?	25
6. Safety Of The Body And Soul	25
What is World View?	28
What is Ideology?	29
Need of study and investigation	29
Principles of World View	30
Search for God	32

Evidences for Existence of God	35
Knowing God According to the Holy Quran	35
A) Verses that Emphasize Contemplation on the Creation of Man	37
B) Verses that Emphasize Contemplation on Creation of Plants, Fruits and Human Foods	39
C) Verses that Emphasize Contemplation on the Importance of Rain and Water	41
Orderliness and Coordination in the World	44
Water Cycle	47
Green Leaves	49
Digestive System	50
Mechanism of Sight	53
Structure of the Eye	53
How Do We See Objects?	56
Adjustment of Image	56
Secondary Organs of the Machinery Of Sight	58
A Discourse on Knowing God	61
Circulatory System	63
First Stage	64
Passage	64
Stage of Narrow Passages	64
Return Journey	65
Entering the Right Atrium	65
Severe Beating	66
Entering the Left Atrium	66
Stages of Heartbeat	66
A Discourse on Knowing God	67
A Glance at the Created World	69
Every Phenomenon has a cause	73
Another Example	74

Law Of Causation Is A Fundamental, Absolute And Universal Law	75
No Effect Is Without Cause	75
World Is Also Having A Cause	76
Explanation of Reasoning About Knowing God	78
Qualities of God	81
Attributes of Perfection	83
Can we imagine God and His Attributes?	85
Can God be Seen?	86
Some Attributes Of Perfection	87
Important Reminder	89
Negative Attributes	90
Oneness of God	95
Monotheism of the Being	96
Oneness in Attributes	97
Oneness in Creation	99
Oneness in Lordship and Will	102
Oneness in Worship	105
Divine Justice	111
The First Proof Is Quran	113
The Second Is Logical Proof	113
Justice in Creation	114
Divine Justice and Objections Against It	119
First: Natural Calamities	120
Second: Children born with physical defects	122
Third: Differences between Individuals	124
Fourth: Existence of Harmful Creatures	125
Role of Justice in Prophethood	127
Effect of Faith on Morals and Good Behavior	136
Morals	138
Worship	138

Foreword

Man is innately curious about 'causes' and it is this same quality that has impelled him to seek the origin or the primary cause of existence. As far as God is concerned, everyone seeks Him in a different way. However, to prove His existence, the Glorious Quran has taught us to use simple but strong reasoning. Among such reasoning, the Quran has put more stress on the 'reasoning of order'. The proof, which is attainable through study and contemplation in the secrets and wonders of creation and the tremendous harmony, concord and consistency embedded in it.

This work, through the 'reasoning of order' deals with theology (knowing god) and oneness, the attributes of God, the different types of oneness and also justice.

This book is part of ideological collection of "Youths and Truths" with topics such as: Knowing God, Resurrection, Prophethood and the Prophet of Islam, Introduction to Islam, Rights and duties of Women, Imamate and the Imams, Youth and Spouse Selection. All these volumes are written by Ayatullah Ibrahim Amini, who has succeeded to author this collection based on years of delving into religious texts and sources, constant contact with the young generation and pondering over ideological and educational issues.

The youth of today looks at the world and then at himself through natural curiosity and inquisitiveness and gradually questions like: 'From have I come?', 'Where am I at present?' and 'Where am I headed?' crop up in his mind; queries that in fact bear the sign of continuous enthusiasm and perpetual clamor of his inner conscience.

Every kind of reply to these queries shapes the beliefs for him and also becomes the basis of all individual and social roles. If his reective queries are replied with materialistic logic, his behavior will take different material shapes or he would develop invalid beliefs, but if it is on the basis of divine logic, all beings for him – from all people and the world – will be having an aim and meaning and the logic will be stretched to perfection of man.

That is why one should be watchful so that the natural and inevitable queries of youth about existence and its aims and after that his duties in this world are answered properly so that he is not deviated and that his natural and mental needs are fullled in the right manner.

Quran and traditions have through logical and sensible replies have made the views of man inclined to take the shape of logical beliefs, Muslim intellectuals have also with the help of these teachings put forth these rm and attractive argumentations and in this manner in the system of Islamic beliefs, basic questions of man, have been given rm and logical replies; but this great scholastic and philosophical heritage, in writings and speeches of people who reect, is sometimes full of technical and complex terms in such a way that it is very difcult to be understood by laymen and especially the youth of today.

His Eminence, Ayatullah Amini,[1] who has for many years, due to his insight of religious texts and sources and his continuous contacts with the youth and concern about their religious and training problems, written a number of books; including the six-volume Youth and beliefs, which is written in a lucid and organized logical manner; comprising of the following: Knowing God, Resurrection, Prophethood and

---

[1] Ustad Ayatullah Ibrahim Amini was born in 1304 Solar year in Najafabad. Having nished his primary studies in Najafabad, he joined the Religious Learning Center of Isfahan. After completing his curriculum of religious studies in Isfahan, he joined the most famous Religious Learning Center of Qom, where he learned jurisprudence and its principles, under the tutorship of most eminent religious scholars of that period: Like Ayatullah Burujardi, Ayatullah Khomeini, Ayatullah Gulpaygani and Muhaqqiq Damaad.

He studied Philosophy under the tutorship of Allamah Tabatabai. In addition to the duties of teaching jurisprudence, its principles and philosophy, he began to write and research from 1342 and most of his books have been published a number of times. Some of them are as follows:

Dad-Gustar -e-Jahan (World Administer of Justice) about the life of Imam al-Mahdi (a.s.); Bano-e-Namuna-e-Islam (The Ideal Woman of Islam), about the life of Fatimeh az-Zahra (s.a.) the daughter of the Holy Prophet (s.a.w.s.); Hame Bayad Be Danand (Everybody should know); A small booklet containing the details of Roots and Branches of the Religion for younger people;

Aayeen-e-Hamsar Dari (the Code of Marital Relationship); Aayeen-e-Tarbiyat dar Tarbiyate-Kudak (The Code of Child- training); Barrasi Masail-e-Kulli Imamat (Overall review of affairs related to Divinely Appointed Vicegerency); Wahy Dar Adyaan Aasmaani (Revelation in Heavenly Religions); Khud Sazi dar Akhlaque (Moral Self-building); Intekhab-e-Hamsar (Selection of Spouse); Islam wa Talim wa Tarbiyat (Education and Training in Islam);

Aashnai ba Masail-e-Kulli Islam (Acquaintance with over all Islamic Affairs); Droos min al-Saqafateh al-Islamiyah (A complete course of Roots and Branches of Religion of Intermediate level); Islam wa Tammudan-e-Gharb (Islam and Western Civilization): Translation from Arabic into Persian of Moududi's Book: Nahn wa al-Hazarate al-Gharbiyeh; Imamaan Ra Behtar Shanaseem (Let us know more about the Imams); Articles on various ideological, political, social, ethical and educational topics for presentation at seminars and conferences. Most of the above books have been translated into one or more foreign languages.

the Prophet of Islam, Knowing Islam, Duties and Rights of Women, Imamate and the Holy Imams (a.s.). Without any doubt, the youth of today can easily derive the replies to all his questions from these books.

Preface

The life of man can be divided into four periods: childhood, youth, middle age and old age. From these, youth is the most sensitive and valuable period, since the child does not reach physical and spiritual stage where he/she can be entrusted with responsibilities; and that is why the responsibility of his control and upbringing is entrusted to the parents. The old age is also the age of weakness, helplessness and needfulness. He should either depend on his savings from the period of his youth or in order to assure them he should depend on his children or assistance from charitable organizations.

Although man in his middle age, has the strength to work and make effort and to fulll the daily needs of his life and has foresight about the needs of his old age, but success in this matter depends on correct use of his youth. Therefore the most sensitive and valuable period of the life of man is his youth.

Physical maturity, bodily strength and mental capacities of the youth reach to such a level that he can with foresight make effort to accept his present and future responsibilities and prepare himself for the future life and his role of a responsible member of society. The special qualities of the youth can be said to be as follows:

Physical tness, bodily strength, constitution, movement, intelligence and strong memory, relaxation and rest, great courage, high hopes, capability of creation and initiative, truthfulness and well-wishing, inner purity and cleanness. Although all youth are not same in having these values, on the contrary there is difference among them, but all of them have these blessings mostly during their youth. The merciful God has blessed youth with all this so that with great courage, foresight and struggle and effort he may obtain success and fortune for himself; but if he is shortcoming in this important thing and wastes his valuable life in carelessness and valuelessness, he would regret it later, when regret would not be of any use.

Amirul Momineen (a.s.) said:

There are two things whose value is not known to man, except after he loses them; youth and health.[2] The Messenger of Allah (S) said:

On Judgment Day, man would not take any step till he is not asked: How did you spend your life and how did you use up your youth?[3]

The Messenger of Allah (S) said to Abu Dharr:

Value ve things before ve others: youth before old age, health before sickness, wealth before poverty, relaxation before being occupied and life before death.[4]

Youths should know the value of youth and they should gain as much as they can from it. And if not they would fall into serious and irredeemable dangers; at that time regret would be of no use. Youths in this particular time have three main responsibilities, which we shall mention in brief below:

First duty: Perfect care about physical tness and health of the body and physical and spiritual faculties. Health is among the greatest divine

---

[2] Ghurarul Hikam, Pg. 414.

[3] Tarikh Yaqubi, Vol. 2, Pg. 90.

[4] Biharul Anwar, Vol. 81, Pg. 173.

bounties and valuable treasure trove of life. Loss of health is the greatest loss; it destroys comfort and pleasure of man and it prevents him from struggle and vigor in achieving great aims.

Imam Ja'far Sadiq (a.s.) said:

There are ve things from which if one loses even one, his whole life would become defective, he would lose his sense and would always be anxious; the rst of them is physical health.[5]

The Messenger of Allah (S) said:

There are two bounties, whose value is not known to man: security and welfare,[6] Amirul Momineen (a.s.) said:

Poverty is a calamity and the worst poverty is physical illness, and the worst physical illness is the disease of conscience.[7]

The youth are specially advised: That they should try to observe hygiene and in nutrition they should be more concerned with fulllment of the needs of the body; they must refrain from eating to satiation. They must also keep away from narcotic substances. They should sleep only as much as is needed. They must never give up exercises and walking. They must also avoid lust and sensual deviations as it leads to damage of your body, nerves and your soul.

Second duty: Determination and planning for the future. Every man should adopt an occupation so that through it he may be able to fulll the needs of his life and that he may live a respectable and successful life and that he may also serve others. He should prepare the causes and prefaces of his future occupation in his youth. The youth can select one of these two paths to enter the society: Either they can choose an independent occupation, which are of numerous kinds.

Although some of them are more or less need practice and skills, but

---

[5] Biharul Anwar, Vol. 81, Pg. 171.

[6] Biharul Anwar, Vol. 81, Pg. 170.

[7] Biharul Anwar, Vol. 81, Pg. 175.

they do not require university education, which requires spending the best days of the life or incurring high expenses. The second option is to get admission in the university and study for degrees in the chosen eld.

After that one should choose a profession, whether it be management, skill based or scientic; although in case he has chosen an appropriate line of work. How nice it would be if in the beginning of their lives all youths choose one of the above paths after keeping in view their physical capabilities, intelligence and memory, family possibilities and their own future after considering the options and through counseling and foresight.

Third duty: Research and study in religious beliefs. The youth who during his childhood has lived in a religious atmosphere at home would naturally be well versed in religious beliefs and habitual in performing religious rituals. Or if he has learnt those things in the religious school for children, after maturity he will recall his past training, which would make him inclined to religion. Now in his youth, he will either look at them with a fresh perspective or avoid them completely.

At that time he would be faced with questions like the following: Where have I come from and who has created me? What was the aim of my creation? Do I have some duties towards my creator, or I am free to do what I like? And if some duties are imposed on me, what are those? From whom should I learn about my duties?

What are its conditions and qualities? Where am I headed and what would my destiny be after death? Would I be answerable for the way I lived in the world? If there exist success and misfortune and reward and punishment in the world after death, what is the path to gain success and avoid misfortune? Such questions and tens like it come upon the clear and illuminated mind of the youth and emphatically demand replies.

Providing correct and satisfactory replies of these questions to the youth is very important and instrumental in shaping his future, because it is through these very replies that the program of life of the youth and after it can be organized and be followed with certainty and he can tread the path of success in life and hereafter and also continue to have peace of mind. But if he fails to obtain the correct replies to these questions, he would fall into very grave and irredeemable dangers and he would regret in the last moments of his life or after death; when regret would be of no use at all.

Therefore, it is most important for the youth to research and study about religious beliefs and to get correct and satisfactory replies; especially in this age when religious beliefs and even their laws are ridiculed at by the enemies of Islam through modern communication techniques and profusion of doubts and objections from every side.

Youth need serious guidance and reliable sources for this research and study and the most important of them are books. Since a long time, fortunate Muslim intellectuals have written numerous good and detailed books on different topics of Knowing God, general and special prophethood, resurrection, laws of philosophy, laws of Imamate, but most of them are difcult for youth, since most of them are in Arabic and others are laces with philosophical and scholastic terms, and are so lengthy that the youth cannot muster enough time to peruse them.

Some of them contain such dubious matters that they tend to make them fall into more doubts. To solve this problem, I have written a series of books of medium level on religious beliefs in accordance with the understanding of youth and time available to them. Books on various topics are prepared in this series: The volumes are Knowing God, Resurrection in Quran, Prophethood and the Prophet of Islam (general and special prophethood), Understanding Islam, Understanding the duties and rights of women and Imamate and the Imams.

In compiling the above titles, the following points were kept in view:

Simple language, brevity and clear reasoning – we have refrained from using difcult philosophical and scholastic arguments. We have also refrained from discussing weak and baseless points. Doubtful and debatable matters are avoided. We have depended mostly on verses of Quran and traditions and tried not to mention unimportant matters.

We hope these books would be really benecial and effective in strengthening religious beliefs of our dear youth.

Ibrahim Amini
10/7/1384

Materialistic and Religious World View; Effects and Consequences

Who am I? Where have I come from? Have I come on my own and would I go away automatically? Or it is someone else who has brought me and he would also take me away? What is my future and where am I headed?…Would death be the end of my life? Or there is life after death as well?…Has this great universe come into being automatically and by accident or it is having a creator? And so on.

Such types of questions arise for every sensible man, especially during the period of youth and he tries to obtain their correct replies and satisfy his curiosity.

Believers and disbelievers have replies to the above question that we present here:

World in the View of Believers

The believer considers the world to be a continuous, arranged and compatible collection, which has not come into being on its own; on the contrary it is created by the wise and powerful creator and it is Him that manages it.

The world with a series of precise laws and stable system has its source in the wisdom and intention of the Almighty Allah, who controls and guards it. And if the favors and blessings of the Almighty Allah had not been there it would not have survived for even a single moment. A believer has faith that the world is an organized and aimed system which has come into existence through the wise command of the Almighty Allah and everything is good in itself and this precise and harmonious system is moving to a higher aim.

In view of a believer man, existing things of the world are needful of a creator for their creation and survival. If the grace of the Almighty Allah had not been there, they would not have come into existence and if His favor had not been there they would not have endured. Due to this, the believer considers every existing thing to be a sign of the grace and mercy of the Lord of the worlds.

End of Life

A believer does not regard death as annihilation and end of life; on the contrary he considers death to be a transfer to the everlasting abode of the hereafter and the beginning of a new everlasting life. The man of faith believes that life in this world is not without aim; on the contrary it is the period of coming and nurturing of the soul and a time for obtaining provisions for the hereafter.

The believer is of the view that the righteous and the wicked are not same and both would denitely see the fruits of their deeds: the Almighty Allah would reward the good deeds of righteous and they would occupy the everlasting abode with perennial happiness in the hereafter. On the other hand, the wicked would also receive the punishment of their vile deeds and have a very difcult life in that world.

The believer considers success of his future as the fruits of his deeds, character, words and good morals and is always trying to prepare the means of his success in the hereafter and makes efforts to keep away from evil and wickedness.

Creator of the Universe

The believer man has faith in the being of the Almighty Allah and considers Him as the creator, owner and controller of all the worlds and creatures. In belief of the faithful, the greatest being, who is known as 'Allah' has created this world and it is Him that administers it and that He is wise, powerful, merciful and eternal. According to the man of belief, Allah is the source of all goodness and perfections.

And that He is absolutely Self-sufcient while the universe and His creatures are always in need of Him. It is Him that protects the universe and creatures and maintains them. It is Him that safeguards the earth and the skies and even if He cuts off His mercy from them for a moment, all of them would be annihilated. He is with everything and everyone and is present everywhere and nothing and no one is equal or like Him.

Prophets

In the view of the believer, prophets are human beings who are absolutely pure and perfect in every aspect and who are chosen to guide mankind to the path of perfection. It is so because the Wise Lord has not abandoned human beings in a condition of perplexity and ignorance. On the contrary, He sent His infallible prophets to them and entrusted them with the program for individual, social, political, material, spiritual and worldly, other-worldly life so that they may guide the human beings and convey to them the life-giving and praiseworthy program.

Where have I come from, where am I at present, and where am I going?

The all-knowing and all-powerful Lord by His grace and kindness has created me in the most beautiful creation (Where have I come from?).

I am in a passing and a changing world, which the wise Lord has created and manages it too. I live in this world so that with the guidance of divine prophets and their successors I may nurture myself and my human morals and perfections and that I should be prepared for the success of an everlasting life and unlimited bounties of the hereafter (Where am I at present?).

I am heading on the path to the world of permanence and perpetuity in the hereafter and there I would be recompensed for my deeds. Death is not the end of life, on the contrary it is transfer from the life of the world and the beginning of another new life (Where am I going?).

Who am I? What duties are imposed on me? What is my origin and who has brought me into existence? Where am I at present and what was the aim of my arrival? Where am I going and what would happen at the end of my life?

As we stated earlier, such questions confront every person and every sensible person through mental effort and his curiosity wants to obtain the correct replies and to satisfy his conscience. Indeed, these questions also confront the non-believers. But they do not contemplate upon them in the proper way; they do not employ their reason and thinking in the right way regarding these basic matters.

Attachment to worldly matters and selsh desires cast a veil on their insight and reason; too much of pleasure seeking keeps them occupied and makes them oblivious of the truth. They avoid contemplating on this important matter and even when they have the opportunity and hear the call of their conscience, they change their mind and even deceive themselves and assure themselves through conjectures. The disbeliever does not have any reply with certainty; on the contrary he only depends on his personal views as follows:

Who am I?

I am an animal who named as 'man' and I am like other beasts. I eat and drink and roam about here and there to fulll my innate desires and needs. I am free from every restriction to satisfy my desires; and as opposed to higher beings, I don't have any responsibility and duty.

Where have I come from?

In reply to this question, the disbeliever says on the basis of his defective notion, that: I am a material being. No one has created me. I have not been created by a conscious creator. I have come into being through coincidence. It is not that a wise and a powerful creator has created me and my creation is aimless and without any purpose.

Where am I?

In a world, which is purely material, aimless and unaware and before existing things, animals and human beings who themselves are created unaware and since I am myself aimless and confused, no awareness and aim is needed either in my creation or in the creation of the world.

Where am I going?

To illness, old age, pain, weakness and nally to annihilation and nothingness. Life in the view of the disbeliever is as follows:

It began with nothing, it grows with unawareness and goes higher and higher till it leaves behind childhood, during the youth his structure is at its peak and the youth lives in the highest fort of life. However, it is a pity that this form and strength is soon a thing of past and after a short time, man falls into decadence, pain and then falls to the lowest level.

Diseases and difculties surround him, the power of youth gradually goes on decreasing and physical faculties reach their end. Eyes, ears and limbs become weak and day by day become useless. The period of the fulllment of base desires comes to an end and the period of weakness and old age begins. Children and friends become unkind and disloyal and leave him alone in his problems…and nally he moves towards nothingness and is buried under dust…

The end of life in the view of the disbeliever is useless, terrible and painful like this. And what a dark end it is! The disbeliever believes that his end is decadence into a horrible nothingness. That is why during his lifetime, he avoids the thought of death and when he is confronted by questions, especially regarding life hereafter and death, he just gives false assurance to himself.

He tries to pacify his mind and conscience through vain pastimes and sensuality; even though they may comfort his nerves only for a short while. However can this stop the inquisitive conscience of man and his curious intellect from asking those questions?

Imagination of uselessness and annihilation and nothingness for the disbeliever is very bitter and painful. These thoughts are like poisonous snakes in his inner being, who continue to sting him and secrete poison and he continues to live in that pain and chastisement. How nice it had been if he had used the faculty of reason and had obtained the right and satisfactory replies.

Fruits of Belief in this Life

Faith in the great creator of the world, who is good, kind; and faith in resurrection and everlasting life in the world of hereafter, after death and faith in prophethood and truth of divine prophets imparts freshness, beauty, purity, illumination and a special sort of contentment. We would mention some of the fruits of faith in the following paragraphs:

1. Hope

A believer, on the basis of faith and the true promises that the Almighty Allah has made to him, his heart is always brimming with hope and anticipation and is always hopeful of His mercy, benecence and kindness. A believer considers Almighty Allah as the most powerful, the most wise and the most kind and therefore during difculties and hardships he seeks refuge from Him and asks Him to fulll his needs and is always in expectation of the unseen help of the Lord.

A believer makes efforts to solve his problems but at the same time he is certain that the Almighty Allah is the helper of believers. A believer does not consider himself to be alone and helpless in the world; on the contrary, he is always full of hope and is certain about receiving divine help. Despair and hopelessness, which are the worst types of circumstances in the world, have no place in the heart of the believer.

Why should he be hopeless when he has faith in a wise and a powerful Lord, who is the owner of the

existing world? Why should he despair when he believes in a God, to whom he is connected; who is the source of all powers, perfections and excellence? He considers such a God as the supporter of men who try to tread the path of truth, well-being and justice and He has faith in their nal success and is always in expectation of it. Since the believer has faith in the grace and unending mercy of Allah, he does not allow himself to fall into despair and hopelessness. And the beautiful effulgence of hope is always alive in him.

But what is the condition of the disbeliever? He has no faith in God, whose refuge he might seek in hardships and difculties; after that he cannot resort to the apparent causes and factors and face of difculties and hardships of his life and he sees himself helpless and without any refuge. He becomes worried and falls into the valley of hopelessness and despair. He considers all to be strangers and considers himself to be despicable, helpless and defeated and despair and hopelessness take hold of his soul like the incurable disease of leprosy.

2. Optimism About The End Of Life

Since the believer has faith in resurrection and the world of the hereafter, he does not fear death and is optimistic about the nal end of his life. A believer has faith that he would not be annihilated with death; on the contrary, he would be transferred from this world to the beautiful and everlasting world of the hereafter.

A believer considers this world as the harvest eld of the hereafter and takes this world to be a place of efforts and struggle and abode of developing human perfections, so that he may become eligible for success in hereafter. For a believer, this world is a place for performing good deeds under the shade of belief in God, and a medium of spiritual maturity and perfection. He considers himself to be responsible and is content that even his smallest deed would not remain without recompense. And that he would receive complete rewards for all his deeds in the hereafter. Nor is a believer afraid of death, on the contrary he considers death in the path of Allah, Jihad for Allah, and martyrdom as the greatest blessing and he accepts it willingly and eagerly, so that he may be able to live forever in the neighborhood of divine mercy and near the righteous servants of the Almighty Allah.

A believer does not consider this life to be aimless and he does not feel any aimlessness; on the contrary, he considers it to be a period of his perfection and self-building and to gain eligibility for success in hereafter. Therefore it is this optimism, which impels him to make efforts to perfect his self to obtain rewards of his good deeds and perfects his self in serving others.

A believer does not consider righteousness, truthfulness, trustworthiness, doing good to others, justice, sacrice, loyalty and other good qualities to be useless. On the contrary he is certain that none of them would be wasted or remain without recompense; and that he would see their results in the hereafter.

But what is the condition of the disbeliever? Is he optimistic about the end of his life? Since the disbeliever has no faith in resurrection, he expects that his life will end in annihilation and nothingness. He considers life to be useless and aimless. In the view of disbelievers, his life began from nothing; he grows and goes higher and higher, leaving childhood behind. And during youth, his physical structure and faculties are is at their peak and the youth lives in the highest point of life.

However, it is a pity that this form and strength is soon gone and after sometime he falls into decadence, pain and to the lowest level. Diseases, difculties and old age come to him one after another and he falls down from the peak into decline and after bearing pains, hardships and old age, nally staggers to nothingness and falls into decadence. His useless body is then buried under the dust. What a horrible end it is! What a useless life it was! Is there anything more terrible than nothingness and annihilation?

During old age, the disbeliever sees that the deeds of all his life are fruitless and useless and no matter how much he tries and laments, he would have to pass away, die and become annihilated. Is it possible for him to be optimistic in such circumstances? How can such a person perform good deeds? For what? And for what purpose? When he has no faith in reward and punishment of the hereafter? In what hope would he do a good turn? How can loyalty, sacrice and martyrdom be justied for such persons?

That is why he is always fearful and worried about death and he cannot have good expectation from it. Because in every moment he is anxious of death – which in his view is annihilation – and which is more painful than hundreds of strikes with an iron rod.

3. Recognition of Duty

Man is always confronted by different problems (individual, social, moral, political and…) that he is compelled to select a stance and decide on a proper reaction to them. If he has faith in religion and correct belief, he derives his duty from that school; he is clear about his duties and had no doubt and hesitation about them at all. If he does not have faith in any school of thought, he would be confused about performing his duties and he would always be pulled here and there.

The believer: He is having servitude (sincere worship) and special submission; he has taken his path, aim and stance from God and His prophets and is following a special program. And in every new circumstance, he derives his duty from the religion of God (divine program) and fullls his duty with optimism, satisfaction and interest; and since he has perfect faith in his chosen path and aim, he makes sacrices in order to fulll his duties and with inclination and eagerness hastens to welcome martyrdom.

A believer considers himself and the whole world to be owned by the Almighty Allah and has faith that since Allah, the Mighty and Sublime has bestowed success and perfection to man, He has sent to him the program of success (religion) through the prophets and has given him the choice to act upon it. A believer has faith that his obedience of laws of religion will convey him to denite success. He considers himself to be having freedom of choice and responsibility of his future and with perfect certainty and without any doubt or perplexity and from the aspect of insight of his duties that he has taken from his religion and school and on which he acts.

However, what is the condition of the disbeliever? Since he did not accept truth and had no faith in any religion, he is always confused and in doubt; he does not know which path to choose and in which direction he should move. He is a prisoner of selsh desires and sensuality; sometimes he is pulled in one direction and sometimes in the other. Whichever way he chooses and whichever work he begins, he has no certainty whether it is in his interest or harmful to him.

He is not able to choose and follow a clear aim which would guarantee his genuine success since he did not accept Allah and the religion of Allah. Other schools deceived him and since he did not accept the right guidance of the prophets and divine saints, he was trapped by imposters, cheaters and liars.

4. Satisfaction

The believer has the cognition of his God and has perfect faith in his knowledge, power, mercy and grace. He considers the Almighty to be master and owner of all existing things and knows that His power and will is in force everywhere. He considers Allah to be present everywhere and that He is aware of everything. A believer has faith that God intends well-being of man and that He is benecent and merciful and never deprives them of His blessings.

That is why he has peace of mind and has no worry and anxiety. The remembrance of God is with him and he is always inclined to Him. The believer has entrusted the boat of his existence to the Almighty Allah and he has faith that He would take him through all whirlpools, horrifying waves and storms and nally give him deliverance. And he is sure to reach the banks of success in the end.

The believer is cognizant of the aim of his life and is condent of his destination that if he walks on that path he would denitely reach his aim and everlasting success. Therefore he has peace of mind and a deep condence in it. Why should he not be condent, when he is having the Almighty Allah as his support; the God who is the source of all goodness? Why should he have any worry, when he is sure that he is having the unseen help of the Lord and that he is not helpless and alone?

But what is the condition of the disbeliever? In his view, this world and its phenomena are like a sea raging with storms, in which waves of hardships of calamites attack from every direction. Neither he has a ship which might save him and nor is there any aware and caring savior for him. The phenomena of the world in his view are unrelated, aimless and haphazard. The disbeliever finds himself to be weak and helpless in this stormy sea and he is surrounded by waves from all sides. He is an exhausted swimmer who does not see any favorable and strong savior; he shakes due to the surging of waves and considers every call to be a call of the enemy and there is nothing with which he can assure himself.

In such a way that he sees himself exposed to death and destruction. How can he rest in peace when the depths of his heart are full of grief, sorrows, defeats, enmities, malice, fear of diseases, poverty, indifference, unkindness, fear of old age and death…? How can the disbeliever have peace? When he has not managed to procure for himself a powerful and favorable refuge for himself in the world on which he could have relied and through which he could have comforted his anxious heart.

Since the disbeliever does not have a true and strong belief, he also does not have a right and determined aim in his life so that he may make continuous efforts in that path. Because he considers himself and worldly phenomena to be aimless, how can he choose a valuable established aim? How can he comfort himself when he believes that the final end would be accompanied with destruction and annihilation? Since the disbeliever has no faith in the world of the hereafter, he sees his future to be dark; he trembles at the thought of death and always lives in anxiety.

5. Patience and Determination

Man, throughout his life is surrounded by difculties, hardships, sorrows, pains, deprivations, failures, illnesses, weakness and…is confronted by the question that how their occurrence affects his life in retributive manner. Some of these phenomena are preventable and some are not, some accidents that occur are such that they are redeemable and some are not and in all these stages and in bearing all these things, the believer and disbeliever would not be same.

The believer, who is supported by strength of faith and gains from guidance of prophets, would be better than others in preventing these accidents and in decreasing their number. In the same way, the believer with regard to events that come to pass and are curable through the help of the unlimited divine power and support of unseen helps, and with patience and forbearance is best to nd the solution of those problems and to make efforts in this regard; from this aspect he is better than others to overpower the difculties and hardships of life.

Since the believer has a clear aim and religious perspective, he makes efforts to fulll his duties in all circumstances and he can be more determined than others in face of hardships and to solve those problems. In this path he is not fearful of any power and is rm like a mountain.

What is the stance of a believer with regard to events which are normally unavoidable? Happenings like old age, incurable diseases, coincidences, unforeseen events, sudden deaths of relatives are common; the religious faith of man makes him steadfast in these calamities. The believer is so patient and forbearing in these circumstances that it seems they are pleasant happenings.

The believer knows that worldly incidents are not without any calculation or program and in case man treads the path of fullling his duties, he can benet from all pleasant and unpleasant events in order to perfect his self and moral qualities to achieve success in the hereafter.

A believer is such that in all these incidents he assumes a stance of absolute serenity and is satised and patient with divine destiny and believes that this patience and satisfaction, along with efforts and struggle would lead to the development of self and maturity of his personal excellences; and he does not pay attention to any harm, because he would be rewarded by the merciful Lord in the hereafter for his patience, contentment, efforts and struggle.

It is due to this faith and belief that a believer welcomes hardships and calamities with open arms and does not complain in any way; he is more stable than a mountain and as much as he can he tries to solve those problems.

Summarily, the believer on the basis of his faith in Allah and the world of hereafter, his faith in divine prophets, and deriving the program of his life from the prophets and their successors, is having the following qualities:

1. He is in control of his passions and selsh desires and is patient; therefore he refrains from actions, which may cause defeat, disgrace and misfortune.
2. With condence that he is having the unseen help of the Lord of the worlds, he is patient in making efforts to fulll his obligations and is patient in his struggles and effort; he confronts the difculties of life with perseverance and steadfastness.
3. He confronts the hardships and tries to solve them with patience and complete steadfastness.
4. In face of extremely serious difculties, he does not lose his self-control and is patient and forbearing for the sake of divine pleasure and proximity to God.

But What Is The Condition Of The Disbeliever?

How can a disbeliever have such patience and steadfastness? When he has not gained from the fruits of the lofty tree of faith; the disbeliever is a captive of base selsh desires and these desires pull him all the time. The disbeliever is degraded before his selsh desires and he cannot control them properly and is unable to gain immunity from deviation. A disbeliever does not have any point of reliance when confronted with hardships that he could be steadfast; and that is why he loses his patience and steadfastness when surrounded by difculties and hardships and despairs of achieving the aim. The disbeliever loses his patience and steadfastness in face of unavoidable difculties, like old age and some diseases and near to death or at the death of his relatives or loss of property. He nds that no avenues is open for him and he falls into grief and sorrow and is seen complaining about it fervently.

Therefore the disbeliever is very much disgusted and anxious when such incidents occur but he cannot do anything.

The disbeliever who had no aim in his life, except the fulllment of base desires, worldly success and eating, drinking and sleeping…how can he remain patient and steadfast in the hardships and sorrows of life that befall everyone?

6. Safety Of The Body And Soul

Since the believer steps forward from the aspect of insight and bases his actions on the foundation of certainty in Allah and truthfulness of His promise he has more peace of mind and is less aficted with diseases of the soul. He does not lose control of himself and does not allow himself to become anxious and worried and as a result, he is safe from some physical diseases, which are also causes of spiritual illnesses. By the strength of faith and attention to values of faith, the cure of believing persons is faster than others, because the soul and body have complimentary inuence on each other.

Moreover, since the believer has access to the rm guidance of divine prophets with regard to the safety of body and soul, he believes in their well-being; he makes use of those instructions and in this way assures the health of his body and soul.

But what is the condition of the disbeliever? Since the disbeliever does not have faith in the wise and powerful God, and considers the existence of his self and the whole world as aimless, he has a feeling of hollowness, aimlessness and confusion. That is why he is not steadfast and does not have contentment of the soul and the most insignicant accident tends to cast him into despair and anxiety and also leads to the worst physical ailments. In the same way, it is possible that weakness of soul may lead to sinfulness so that he may conceal his inner worry and apprehension. The disbeliever is more prone to diseases of the soul, anxiety and inner apprehension as well as physical diseases.

Also, the disbeliever does not have faith in guidance of prophets based on the rm message of God with regard to physical and spiritual health and the most benecial manners that believers usually follow.

They have no faith in them; therefore they give up hope in face of problems and hardships and most fall into diseases of the soul or the body.

The period of youth and maturity is a very sensitive and crucial period for making the future. As if it is a period of the beginning of a new life. In this stage, the intellectual capacity and thinking power develops leading to rm beliefs in the future. And the youth should be sensitive for the future during this period and they should chalk out a plan for themselves. Losing this valuable opportunity would make them suffer an irredeemable harm, because the opportunity passes and the age which has gone by does not ever come back.

Man is a sensible being having foresight and he cannot, like pure beasts, follow his selsh desires. He is supposed to make use of his reasoning ability and should identify his duties in this world. He must follow the path of humanity and achieve his real success. A man with intelligence and foresight does not waste the valuable opportunity of his life, but considers two things necessary for himself and tries to achieve them: thirdly correct belief, organized and accounted program.

The youth is supposed to use this opportunity, and to identify the real aim of life and make a rm determination for his future; he should tread the path of his actual success and should walk on it with awareness and perfect insight; and he should make efforts to fulll his aim.

But it is clear that choosing a proper program and precise path of success depends on the belief and world view of a person. Every person with regard to cognition and belief about the world would identify the aim of life and the path that he should tread and he should determine the future and make a program for it. As much perfect and correct are our cognitions about the basic problems of the world of existence, we can recognize the aim of life in a better way and can make efforts to act according to that program in the best way. On the other hand, if our cognition about the basic matters of the world of existence (world view) are wrong and we harbor invalid beliefs, we would make a mistake in selecting the aim and path and also the program of the future and would fall into the bottomless abyss of destruction.

Therefore, the rst need for a man of foresight is to strengthen the basis of beliefs and a right world view. Every sensible person needs that in the rst stage of life in his youth, he should work towards strengthening his beliefs and he should through reasoning and evidences make the basis of his faith strong. And through this he can save himself from confusion, perplexity and deviation.

Basically research and curiosity in exposing the secrets of the world is in the nature of a man with insight. How can he ignore these natural desires and how can he satisfy his intellect? If he doesn't, what would be his superiority over other beasts?

What is World View?

Recognition and imagination that man is from the world of existence is called as 'world view'. In other words, 'world view' is that which provides proper replies to the following fundamental matters:

Has this world come into existence automatically or a higher being has created it and which controls it? If it has a creator, what type of existence does He have? What qualities are present in Him? What is the aim in creating man and the world? Is the life of man permanent in this world or it is as such in another world that is the world of the hereafter where man is transferred after death, so that he may recompensed for his deeds and behavior? What type of a world is hereafter, Paradise and Hell? What type of an existing being man is? And what capacities are present in him? Does man have duties and responsibilities in this world…?

Can man, in order to secure success of his world and hereafter arrange a perfect program? Or it is necessary for him to follow divine guides and programs of prophets having contacts with divine revelation? What type of persons the prophets are and what qualities do they have? And…?

Whether there is need of a person who is aware and powerful and supported by prophet and Almighty Allah to assure correct application of laws and rules of religion, guidance of people, guarding the social system, maintaining justice in society and survival of the path of prophets?

Reply of people to these types of question is not similar. On the contrary every group will give their special reply according to its belief and world view. Their total replies shapes a system of thinking, which is named as world view.

What is Ideology?

After selection of the world view it is the turn of ideology.[8] Terminologically, ideology implies an organized and aimed program and a perfect guideline of life and a system of thinking which determines the duties of man.

Therefore the term, 'world view' is the foundation and ideology is its product; that is selection of an ideology depends on selection of a world view. In fact, world view is complete recognition with regard to existence; but ideology means recognition and awareness of duties, dos and don'ts and values.

Replies to such questions are called as ideology in terminology:

What is our duty in this world? What responsibility do we have? In what act does the success and real perfection of man lies? What are good deeds and what are bad deeds? And…?

In what actions does the well-being of man lie? Which acts should we perform and which should we leave?…?

Need of study and investigation

Such questions arise for all curious youths, intellectual, wisdom seekers and seekers of truth and demand appropriate replies. Youths, during the period of inquisitiveness and research and during the development

---

[8] Ideology consists of two Latin words: Idea+ logy. Idea is in the meaning of view, belief and imagination. Logy is in the meaning of identity and study. Therefore ideology means the cognition of beliefs and views and study into religious beliefs.

Nowadays in addition to its usual meaning it is also used in the sense of a system of views that people have about every aspect of human life. 1. It almost means same as world view. 2. System of thinking which is a guideline for life of man and which specifies the dos and don'ts and values and that is why it is considered to be an effect of the world view. In this book we have used the word of ideology in this sense.

of their opinions and views are in the stage of concluding their faith and belief. That is why it is necessary that during this period, they should have correct view about the world and should strengthen their beliefs. They should use their foresight, make investigations and derive satisfactory replies to all such questions.

Therefore, it is most necessary to obtain a correct and denite world view and a clear and a rm ideology. Since you are sensible and have foresight and the inquisitive intellect does not allow you to ignore these fundamental matters; passing over these matters in a cursory manner would lead man to fall into confusion and perplexity and makes his life a dreadful abyss of futility and perplexity.

Principles of World View

Let us once again revise the questions that arise in the discussion of world view. We can divide such questions into five groups:

1. Questions related to the beginning of existence and creator of universe and His qualities, and this discussion is called 'Knowing God'.
2. Questions related to the future of man and life after death that is called as 'Knowledge of resurrection'.
3. Questions related to needs of man of an organized program and need for prophets and need of leadership and their guidance; which is called as knowledge of prophethood or messengership.
4. Questions related to the need of man for guides of the Almighty Allah, whose existence is necessary for organization of an equitable society, guarding and application of heavenly laws and guiding people. This discussion is named as knowledge of recognizing the Imam.
5. Questions related to programs, duties and religious responsibili-

ties, which are sent through prophets.

Search for God

Even history clearly shows and it can be concluded through research and investigation also that the man of the past and even pre-historic man was aware of a higher being (who is named as God or any other name) and he humbled before Him and worshipped Him and performed various rituals to seek His pleasure.

Now the question arises, that how man in the beginning became attentive to God? What was the cause that turned his thinking to God? Which factor made him inclined to go out in search of the creator of universe? What is the aim and cause of this view? Basically which factor was effective in compelling man to think about God and God-worship and to contemplate on these lines?

Replies to these questions are possible if one puts in a little effort: Human beings possess an instinct called as the instinct of nding out the cause of every phenomenon. Since the rst day, man was aware of causation and he searched for the cause of every phenomenon and every needful existing being. If he became hungry, he went in search of food, because he considered eating as a cause of removal of hunger. If he became thirsty, he went in search of water, as he considered drinking water to be the cause of removing thirst. If he heard a sound from behind the wall, he became certain that it had a cause and went to find it. If he fell ill, he knew that it was as a result of a cause and he went out in search of its cure. In order to escape cold, he took refuge with heat, since he considered heat to be the cause of removing cold.

Seeking the cause and inquisitiveness is placed in the nature of all human beings. Every man is always trying to become aware of causes. Therefore, with regard to every phenomenon, the question, "Why and for what reason" arises. He always tries to satisfy his sense of curiosity through satisfactory replies.

Man is basically a 'seeker of cause' and he cannot give up this instinct or ignore it. All human beings – especially the earliest man – were having this natural instinct. Man lived in this world and was confronted by incidents and astonishing phenomena; the change of days and nights, summer and winter, movement of moon, sun and stars, peculiarities of animals and plants, lofty mountains, vast seas, owing water bodies…he saw all of this with his eyes and fell into contemplation and asked himself: What is the cause of this world and who has brought it into existence? This universe must definitely be having a cause and the wise and powerful creator has created it and He is controlling it.

In this way, the earliest man became cognizant of Almighty Allah and confessed to his existence, and humbled himself before His greatness and in brief it can be said that seeking God is in the nature of man.

Although a group has fallen into doubts and became involved in worship of false deities and gradually sun worship, moon worship, fire worship and star worship…also appeared in human beings.

However the appearance of false deities is itself proof that man paid attention to his innate nature of seeking cause and concluded that a cause was necessary to control this world. But he fell into misunderstandings with regard to other aspects and considered false gods to be the cause and considered them as true creators, and became involved in their adoration.

In short, it can be said that man searches for the cause of all existing things and phenomena through natural instinct placed in his nature and in this way, he reaches up to Almighty Allah, who is the nal cause of all things and One to whom all are needful. In this way, His being is revealed to them and they begin to worship Him. Quran also considers seeking God to be an innate nature and says:

"And if you should ask them, Who created the heavens and the earth? they would most certainly say: The Mighty, the Knowing One, has created them..." (43:9)

And says:

"And if you ask them, Who created the heavens and the earth and made the sun and the moon subservient, they will certainly say, Allah. Whence are they then turned away?" (29:61)

Then He says:

"And if you ask them Who is it that sends down water from the clouds, then gives life to the earth with it after its death, they will certainly say, Allah. Say: All praise is due to Allah. Nay, most of them do not understand." (29:63)

Evidences for Existence of God

Knowing God According to the Holy Quran

The Holy Quran has used many simple and very basic techniques to prove the existence of God; methods, which are nice as well as easy to understand for everyone. This style is not complex and difcult like the reasonings employed by philosophy, that it may not be understood by all. This most simple method does not require prefaces and advanced learning.

Every person can benet from it in accordance with his or her awareness and knowledge. That simple and beautiful method is called as 'evidence of order' that awakens the innate natures of seeking God. Therefore study and contemplation on the secrets and peculiarities of the created world is one of the best ways of knowing God.

In a large number of verses, Quran has mentioned examples of the astonishing aspects of universe and wants man to think in the right way and to conclude the existence and being of the Almighty Allah from the order and compatibility. According to Quran, each phenomenon of the world is a divine sign (Ayah). Ayah implies a sign or a mark. If man sees the phenomena of the world as they are, he would begin to believe in existence of their creator; although Quran is not a book of natural science that it may discuss secrets of the phenomena of the world in detail and expose them to man. But it has mentioned in brief their astonishing aspects only to prove the existence of the maker of Universe so that it may awaken the minds of those who have the faculty of thinking; and that it may call their attention so that they may discuss and be curious about the exposition of astonishing secrets of Nature and in this way they may begin to have faith in the creator of the world. In addition to this, they may also benet to secure the needs of life and inhabit the world.

That is why it can be said that the science of knowing man, knowing animals, knowing plants, knowing lands, knowing space, physics and chemistry are the best ways to know God.

In the Holy Quran, there are numerous verses which mention examples of the astonishing aspects of creation which awaken the nature of man to seek God, so that he may begin to have belief in the existence of a wise and a powerful creator through his conscience. So that he may see the creator of the world with the eyes of his conscience and that he may become attached to Him. These verses can be divided into different groups and each of them talk of one particular aspect:

A) Verses that Emphasize Contemplation on the Creation of Man

The Almighty Allah says in the Quran:

> *"So let man consider of what he is created: He is created of water pouring forth, Coming from between the back and the ribs." (86:5-7)*

And He says:

> *"And one of His signs is that He created you from dust, then lo! you are mortals (who) scatter. And one of His signs is that He created mates for you from yourselves that you may nd rest in them, and He put between you love and compassion; most surely there are signs in this for a people who reect." (30:20-21)*

And He says:

> *"And one of His signs is the creation of the heavens and the earth and the diversity of your tongues and colors; most surely there are signs in this for the learned. And one of His signs is your sleeping and your seeking of His grace by night and (by) day; most surely there are signs in this for a people who would hear." (30:22-23)*

And He says:

> *"And Allah has brought you forth from the wombs of your*

mothers – you did not know anything – and He gave you hearing and sight and hearts that you may give thanks." (16:78)

And He says:

"We have created you, why do you not then assent? Have you considered the seed? Is it you that create it or are We the creators?" (56:57-59)

And He says:

"There surely came over man a period of time when he was a thing not worth mentioning. Surely We have created man from a small life-germ uniting (itself): We mean to try him, so We have made him hearing, seeing." (76:1-2)

Points

Important points are mentioned in the above verses for man to contemplate on:

1. Previously man was nothing, except a mixed sperm, which underwent various stages to nally assume the shape of man. This process is worth contemplation and study.
2. Human beings are created in pairs so that they might reproduce and also derive comfort from each other; and God has put love and mercy amongst them, which is one of the divine signs.
3. He created human beings in various colors and races, who speak different languages and this is also a remarkable sign and it is worth contemplation.
4. In the beginning man was not aware of anything and he leant

everything from eyes, ears and other senses and conscience. And this too is an astonishing sign worth contemplation and study.
5. Sleep, rest and willingness to obtain livelihood is also a great divine sign.

If man looks at his beautiful structure and ponders well on the extraordinary system and its astonishing aspects, he would conclude that it has not come into being on its own by coincidence. On the contrary it has a wise and a powerful creator.

B) Verses that Emphasize Contemplation on Creation of Plants, Fruits and Human Foods

The Almighty Allah says in the Holy Quran:

> *"And He it is Who sends down water from the cloud, then We bring forth with it buds of all (plants), then We bring forth from it green (foliage) from which We produce grain piled up (in the ear); and of the palm-tree, of the sheaths of it, come forth clusters (of dates) within reach, and gardens of grapes and olives and pomegranates, alike and unlike; behold the fruit of it when it yields the fruit and the ripening of it; most surely there are signs in this for a people who believe." (6:99)*

And He says:

> *"And in the earth there are tracts side by side and gardens of grapes and corn and palm trees having one root and (others) having distinct roots – they are watered with one water, and We make some of them excel others in fruit; most surely there are signs in this for a people who understand." (13:4)*

And He says:

> *"Then let man look to his food, that We pour down the water, pouring (it) down in abundance, then We cleave the earth, cleaving (it) asunder, then We cause to grow therein the grain, and grapes and clover, and the olive and the palm, And thick gardens, And fruits and herbage, a provision for you and for your cattle." (80:24-32)*

And He says:

> *"Have you considered what you sow? Is it you that cause it to grow, or are We the causers of growth? If We pleased, We should have certainly made it broken down into pieces, then would you begin to lament." (56:63-65)*

And He says:

> *"Who made the earth for you an expanse and made for you therein paths and sent down water from the cloud; then thereby We have brought forth many species of various herbs. Eat and pasture your cattle; most surely there are signs in this for those endowed with understanding." (20:53-54)*

Points

Some very important points are mentioned in the above verses also so that man may ponder over them:

1. Man is in need of different types of foods, and vegetation and plants guarantee this need and produce food for him.
2. Plants depend on water for their own growth, which falls from

the sky as rain.
3. Although trees and shrubs grow from the same earth and use the same water, they produce different kinds of fruits and grains.
4. Plants, like animals are also created in pairs.
5. Creation of fruits, grains, vegetables are remarkable and deserve contemplation and attention. In these verses, Quran has called attention to the world of plants and vegetation to highlight astonishing aspects of the plant kingdom so that all may become aware of God creator and that they may benet from them and their fruits.

C) Verses that Emphasize Contemplation on the Importance of Rain and Water

The Almighty Allah says in the Holy Quran:

> *"Most surely in the creation of the heavens and the earth and the alternation of the night and the day, and the ships that run in the sea with that which prots men, and the water that Allah sends down from the cloud, then gives life with it to the earth after its death and spreads in it all (kinds of) animals, and the changing of the winds and the clouds made subservient between the heaven and the earth, there are signs for a people who understand." (2:164)*

And He says:

> *"Have you considered the water which you drink? Is it you that send it down from the clouds, or are We the senders? If We pleased, We would have made it salty; why do you not*

then give thanks?" (56:68-70)

And He says:

"Allah is He Who created the heavens and the earth and sent down water from the clouds, then brought forth with it fruits as a sustenance for you, and He has made the ships subservient to you, that they might run their course in the sea by His command, and He has made the rivers subservient to you." (14:32)

Points

1. These verses describe the beautiful water cycle in nature. The water in oceans evaporates through heat of sun and appears in the sky in form of clouds; and then through the movement of the winds, is transferred to different parts of the earth, where it falls in form of rain and becomes available for human beings, animals and plants. This is one of the divine signs that He has created such a novel system.
2. Although sea water is saline and bitter, rain water is sweet and potable.
3. Water, which is the nectar of life for plants, animals and human beings; was created as a liquid, so that it may ow in the form of streams to be made available for all and also used as mode of transportation (shipping).

Creation of water and its cycle in nature is one of the amazing signs of His creation and for those who have sense, it is worth contemplation; and the order, coordination and connection between human beings, animals, plants, heat of the sun, wind and earth show that these are the best evidences of the existence of a wise and powerful creator.

Orderliness and Coordination in the World

Look at a book; it consists of millions of letters and thousands of words, all of them in a proper arrangement. What is the relation between these letters and words? Are they placed haphazardly besides each other without any system? Or they are arranged in a systematic manner?

After you read the book, you conclude that all the letters, words, sentences and different sections of it are perfectly connected to each other and appropriately placed one after another in order to achieve a single aim. These letters and words are arranged in a particular way and each of them has a peculiarity. You will understand well that an aim was followed in arrangement and compilation of these letters and words.

You will also realize that the compiler of the book possessed intellect and understanding and was previously aware of his work and he arranged the letters and words with foresight and aim in this particular way; and that he is an expert of his eld. In an organized collection, each of its parts is related to others and follows a single aim. Every part is having a particular position and function, that if it is placed in another place or does not perform its function, its job would remain incomplete and the intended aim would not be realized.

Can you have the feeling that it came into being on its own coincidentally without any aim? Can you imagine that an existing being without sense and perception – for example the wind – has pulled the pen across the paper and this book was produced through this process? You can never imagine that the book came into being automatically without an objective and cannot in any way presume that it came into existence through a thing lacking sense and perception and it coincidentally took the shape of this book. Because you know that every phenomenon has an appropriate cause and if someone was to make such a supposition, you would laugh at him and consider his statement senseless. Therefore the presence of the book and systematic arrangement of its words lead us to conclude the following:

Firstly, that the book is having a writer or a compiler.

Secondly, that the writer is wise, intelligent and expert in his eld and that he followed a particular aim in his work.

In the same way, every orderly and aimed mechanism leads you to conclude that it has a wise and an aware maker and as much complex that machine, as much would be the capability of its maker.

The great book of creation is also having letters, words and sentences; every existing thing and phenomenon are words and sentences of this great book. Occurrences and phenomenon of the world are not haphazard and random, on the contrary like letters and words of the book; they have order and coordination throughout. In this great book, you would see that in the structure of human body, which is a book of creation, there are hundreds of systematic and orderly mechanisms and in the structure of each of them you would see precision and accuracy. This system is made up of various organs that work in unison. They cooperate with each other and fulll the needs of each other. Every system of the human body is like a huge workshop. And all these workshops are connected to each other. All the physical organs of man work in order and coordination, so that man can continue to live.

Human body also is unable to survive all by itself. On the contrary, it depends on various other existing things like water, air and different types of nourishments; trees, plants and animals; and also various natural minerals of the earth. He cannot live without them and he is also dependent on the heat and light of the sun, the orderly movement of the earth and the rotation of the days and night and the different seasons.

So much so, that you would say that all of them shape a single real entity in which perfection, organization and compatibility is maintained. Look at this great book of creation; that is this world, carefully and take note of its searching and beautiful words; you would denitely see coordination and system in them. What do you see? You would well understand that this great creation has not come into being by coincidence and without any objective. Senseless and imperceptive Nature could not have brought into existence such a precise system. It cannot write such a meaningful and aimed book.

By looking at the world and by understanding its connection and coordination, you would nicely be able to discover its actual cause. You would conclude the world is a creation of a wise and powerful being, who created it with a particular aim and who is also controlling it. You would see this system everywhere; every phenomenon you study, you will become aware of the knowledge and power of the God, creator of the world. And this way of looking and pondering is the best way to recognize God; and it is called as the evidence of order.

Numerous verses of Quran emphasize contemplation on the creation of the earth and the heavens, sun and stars, animals and plants, systematic appearance of day and night, physical development of man, differences of colors, faces and languages in order to discover the creator of the world.

Water Cycle

Distribution of water between existing things is very remarkable and amazing. The real sources of water are the seas, oceans and lakes. Water is distributed throughout the earth from these bountiful sources.

Water of oceans, seas and lakes, under the effect of the heat of sun, turns to vapor and rises to the sky. Vapors wander in sky with the movement of winds. When temperature and pressure reach a particular level, they appear in form of clouds and oat to various parts of the earth by the movement of fast and slow winds, where they drop as rain, soaking up the earth and giving rise to vegetation and greenery. Rain water then seeps into the earth and is stored in it for needful times. The stored water sometimes erupts from the lap of mountains in form of springs or human beings make efforts to dig wells and gain from the life-giving sources of water in the earth.

Drops of rain, in special circumstances, fall to the ground slowly and beautifully in form of snow. Snow which is very benecial for vegetation as it turns into water gradually and seeps into the earth and is stored underground or emerges as springs and rivers and becomes available for those who need it and in the end return to the seas.

The quality of the rising of vapor and its being transferred from one place to another by the help of wind itself deserves contemplation. If wind power had not been there, how the clouds would have been distributed in the atmosphere? How they would have traveled here and there? If the heat of the sun had not been there, would the water of the sea have turned into vapor? If the water had only turned into vapor at temperature of a hundred degrees, would it have been sufcient for existing beings? Would human life have been possible in those circumstances? If rain had not fallen down in drops, what difculties it would have brought? For example, if rain fell from the sky in one place in form of a stream, what would happen? Would it have been able to seep into the earth in a gradual manner and be stored in it?

Quality of rain and snow in purifying the atmosphere is also remarkable and worth pondering. If rain and snow had not absorbed the toxins and dirt of the atmosphere, would you have been able to breathe?

Now you must have noted what valuable qualities are present in water, snow and rain. How the sea and sun, wind and cloud and rain etc. act in a precise coordinated way to provide means of life for us and other existing things.

What does this system and coordination prove? Is it not the best proof that intelligence and determination had a role in the creation of this magnicent world? Does this system and coordination not tell us that a wise and a powerful being has created this world? And that He created man and other existing things and all that they need?

Now, that we have mostly understood well the value, importance and qualities, we must see what the Almighty Allah has xed as our duty before these bounties. He has commanded us to enjoy the benets of these bounties and be obedient and thankful to Him. That we drink it and give to others; that we may purify ourselves and our surroundings through it. We should take care that we must not waste it, that we should be thrifty in using water so that others may not have to face its shortage. We must not pollute rivers, streams, seas and sea shores. We should try to save underground water bodies and use this great divine bounty in a nice way, on which human, animal and plant life depends to populate the earth and to guarantee the needs of all.

The Almighty Allah says in the Holy Quran:

"...and We have made of water everything living." (21:30)

And He says:

"Allah is He Who sends forth the winds so they raise a cloud,

then He spreads it forth in the sky as He pleases, and He breaks it up so that you see the rain coming forth from inside it; then when He causes it to fall upon whom He pleases of His servants, lo! they are joyful." (30:48)

And He says:

"He it is Who sends down water from the cloud for you; it gives drink, and by it (grow) the trees upon which you pasture. He causes to grow for you thereby herbage, and the olives, and the palm trees, and the grapes, and of all the fruits; most surely there is a sign in this for a people who reect." (16:10-11)

Green Leaves

All of us require food and we cannot survive or work without nourishment. Trees and plants prepare food for us. The green leaves of plants are small food-making workshops; they work and produce food for us.

Plants and trees obtain water and minerals from soil through roots and transport them to the leaves through stems.

Carbon dioxide also, which is present in the atmosphere enter the leaves through numerous tiny pores and light and solar energy also heats up the leaves.

At that time, the workshop of green leaves starts working and prepares food with the help of the sun.

Plants produce more food than what is required for their own use; they use some of it and the rest is stored for us.

Sheep and cows also require food and they graze on green grass and feed on grains and produce for us milk, cheese and meat. Fowls also feed on grain and produce eggs and chicken for us.

All animals and beasts are in need of plants and the food of all of them is prepared through green plants. No human being or animal can produce their food without the help of plants. All are in need of plants.

Human beings are in need of plants and animals, and animals require plants and plants require water, soil, carbon dioxide and sunlight to prepare the food.

Now let us see who has created the sun, so that it may shine on the earth and distribute light and energy for the plants to produce food for us. Who has created these systematic and coordinated trees and plants and given to the green leaves the power of producing food?

That wise and powerful being is God, who is all knowing and all powerful.

That wise and powerful creator loves us so much that through foresight He has created everything that we might ever need. We also love Him; we thank Him for His bounties, accept His guidance and follow them – who can guide our life better than Almighty God?

Digestive System

We require food for health, survival, movement and work. Materials required by our body are present in the foods that we eat. But most of them are not absorbed into our body in their original form; on the contrary they have to be digested. Digestion is the process of breaking up the food that we eat into a form that can be absorbed into our body to produce nourishment.

And this important function is performed through the digestive system. Digestive system consists of a tube which begins from the mouth and ends at the last outlet (anus). Passing through this small workshop, food undergoes hundreds of thousands processes and ne and amazing reactions and becomes digested and absorbable. So many elaborate processes take place, which can hardly be described over here.

Some of them are mentioned by way of examples.

We shall divide the digestive tract into parts and explain the function of each part in brief.

Mouth: Some organs are present in the mouth which are effective in digestion: lips, tongue, teeth (in particular way), jaws and three pairs of salivary glands.

When the morsel enters the mouth, the lips close the entrance so that the food may not fall out. The tongue rotates in the mouth and places the morsel under the teeth. The lower jaw moves up and down so that the morsel may be chewed and become soft. All this time, the salivary glands secrete liquids and enzymes on the surface of the morsel so that it may help in digestion. Secretion of salivary glands continues at other times also and keeps the tongue and lips moist to facilitate speaking and breathing and also to help in the sense of taste.

Throat and the process of swallowing: Three passages are present in the gullet, the nasal tube, respiratory tube and the food tract, which is connected to the stomach. Food must not enter the air tube or it would disrupt breathing and we would choke. When the morsel in the mouth is ready to be swallowed, the tongue gathers it and sends it to the throat. At that same time the uvula is raised and closes the nasal tube. The air tube is also closed by the epiglottis. The only thing open at that moment is the food tube and the morsel enters it and by the worm like movements is propelled to the stomach.

Circular muscles in the last part Esophagus (cardia) is normally contracted and it prevents the stomach juices from entering the esophagus, but on receiving worm-like motions to this end, the contraction of muscles goes away and the entry of food to the stomach is facilitated.

Stomach: The food matter remains in the stomach for a period of time. Different types of foods stay in the stomach for different lengths of time. After the food enters the stomach, weak contractions appear in its muscles. They become stronger and more frequent gradually. These contractions in the form of worm-like waves begin from below (cardia) and throughout the length of the stomach travel to the pyloric sphincter, and as they reach the pyloric sphincter they become stronger and causing the softening of food matter and its mixing with the gastric juices.

There are numerous glands in the inner wall of the stomach that secrete enzymes and special liquids on the surface of the food; with this action starch is converted into glucose and protein is changed to amino acids. Also the food matter is converted into smaller particles t to be absorbed by the different cells of the body. The food matter through these actions and reactions assumes the form of a paste, which is called as chime and after that it gradually enters the duodenum.

Duodenum: The initial part of the small intestine is called duodenum. When the food enters the small intestine, it rst passes through the duodenum and at this place through pancreas and gall bladder liquids are sprayed on its surface, which affect digestion of food in a systematic manner.

Small intestine: The food does not stay in the small duodenum; on the contrary it passes through it into the small intestine. Matter resultant from digestion of food through the small intestine is absorbed and enters the blood stream, so that with the circulation of blood it may come at the disposal of all the cells of the body. The inner surface of the small intestine has numerous folds through which the digested food is absorbed into the blood stream and transferred to the liver.

Large intestine: The large intestine is the last part of the digestive tract. When food enters the large intestine no useful or absorbable matter remains in it. Things that remain behind in it are a quantity of water, salts and a little undigested food matter. The walls of the large intestine absorb the water and salts and in the end, half solid excrement including dead and alive bacteria and indigestible matter remains in the rectum till it is excreted through the anus.

Mechanism of Sight

Even now as you read this book you are concerned with eyes and are completely aware of their value and existence. But perhaps till now you have not rightly thought about the construction of this small but complex and delicate organ of sight. The eye is one of the most beautiful and amazing signs of Almighty Allah; such that by studying it and pondering on the process of its creation, it is possible to discover the existence of the wise and powerful God, who is the creator of the world; and to become cognizant of the unlimited aspects of knowledge and power. There are so many amazing aspects of the human eye that it is not possible to mention all of them in this book. But we shall indicate some of them here. First of all let us become aware of the structure of the eye ball and after that we can take up the discussion of knowing God.

Structure of the Eye

The eye ball is the real instrument of seeing, which works like a camera – on the contrary more complex than a camera. The eye ball is made up of three layers: sclera, choroids and retina.

1. What is the Sclera? It is a veil which is hard, rm, white and turbid and is approximately one millimeter thick. It covers the complete eye ball and protects it. Front of this sheet (sclera) is transparent in order to allow light to enter the eye. It is known as the cornea.
2. What is the Choroid? It is a thin and black curtain inside the sclera and which changes the interior of the eye into a dark chamber. Inside the choroid are a large number of blood veins which supply

nutrition to eye structures and in fact choroids is also the food giving layer of the eye. The front portion of the choroid is in the form of a circular curtain xed behind the cornea and which is known as iris.

There is an aperture in the center of iris, three to six millimeters in diameter and it is known as the pupil. The pupil automatically enlarges and contracts to regulate light entering the eye.

1. What is the retina? Retina is innermost sensitive layer of the eye. Images of bodies which come before the eye fall upon this curtain; the inner surface of the retina is the rst colored layer. A jelly like substance called vitreous humor lls the space between lens and retina. The lens, iris and cornea are nourished by a clear uid, aqueous humor, formed by the ciliary body and which lls the space between lens and cornea. Two types of receptors – rods and cones – are present. Rods are mainly found in the peripheral retina and enable us to see in dim light and to detect peripheral motion.

They are primarily responsible for night vision and visual orientation. Cones are principally found in the central retina and provide detailed vision for such tasks as reading or distinguishing distant objects. They also are necessary for color detection. These photoreceptors convert light to electrochemical impulses that are transmitted via the nerves to the brain. Rods are approximately 120 million and cones are ve million in number.

The uid ows from ciliary body to the pupil and is absorbed through the channels in the angle of anterior chamber. The delicate balance of aqueous production and absorption controls pressure within the eye. Optical nerves connect the retina to the brain.

Yellow spot – at the rear of the eyeball there is a depression on the retina wall ellipse in shape and it is one millimeter in diameter and called as the Yellow spot. The Yellow spot is exactly in line of the pupil and it focuses the light that falls on it. Yellow spot is a part of retina and is its most sensitive portion and conical cells are compressed here in concentration and each of them is connected through a nerve to the center of sight in the brain. In order to see bodies clearly, our eyes automatically circle the surface of that body whose image falls on the Yellow spot.

Transparent Mantles of the Eyeball

Transparent mantles of the eyeball are parts which allow light to pass through them and which focus on the surface of retina. These transparent mantles are as follows: Cornea, Aqueous humor, lens and Vitreous body.

1. Cornea: It is the same frontal part of the sclerotic, which is foremost and transparent.
2. Aqueous humor: It is a transparent liquid, which lls up the space between cornea and lens.
3. Lens: It is a body, which is curved at both the ends and is present in the front portion of the eye and behind the iris. It is better that you know that the lens is suspended with the help of suspension ligaments and is joined to the choroid and conceals the surface of the lens with a delicate, transparent and adjustable veil called as crystalloid. The lens is composed of long cord-like cells and some of them even have nucleus. The lens cords are hard and concentrated and they form the nucleus of the lens.
4. Vitreous body: It is a transparent matter, which lls the inner space of the eyeball and is partly condensed in the form of a delicate curtain.

How Do We See Objects?

From the bodies that are placed before our eyes, rays of light are reected to our eyes; these rays cross the cornea and enter the lens through the pupil. They pass the lens as well till they are reected on the Yellow spot at the rear of the eyeball on the surface of retina. In this manner their image, which is reected and reduced in size falls on sensitive conical cells of the Yellow spot. These cells convey the image through optical nerves to the centre of sight in the brain. The soul or the self of man in this way is able to see objects through this process and reactions and it can become aware of the color, volume and distance of those objects.

Adjustment of Image

You know that objects are clearly visible only if their image falls exactly on the Yellow spot, neither behind it nor in front of it. In ordinary circumstances the lens can throws a clear image of anything that is at a distance of six meters or more on the most sensitive part of the eye that is the Yellow spot. But the lesser the distance of the object to eye, the lesser would be its visibility as its image would fall much behind the Yellow spot and hence that object would not be seen clearly.

But according to the plan that is in force in the creation of the eye, this difculty has been solved in a beautiful manner, in the way that curvature of the lens is changeable. A healthy and normal eye automatically adjusts the curvature of its lens according to the distance of the object whose image it wants to focus on retina. If the distance of the object is lesser than normal the curvature of also increases in accordance with it so that its image falls exactly on the Yellow spot. In such a way: that ciliary muscles exert pressure on the eye and this causes the suspensory ligaments to be elongated as a result of which the surrounding of the lens is stretched and in its middle it is having a hard nucleus, which does not allow the stretching beyond a certain point. In order to see the near objects, the thickness of the lens increases as a result of which the distance of its focus changes and in order to see objects at a distance its thickness decreases. This process is known as focusing. It is one of the most minute and swift action of the eye, which is performed during the seeing of objects. In every moment that we see around us and see the near and far scenes and things, our lens changes its thickness hundreds of times in succession and we see all the objects nicely and clearly. Have you so far paid attention to these minute actions of the eye?

We know that this small body is composed of hundreds of smaller organs and millions of different types of cells and each of them have a special function and they perform these functions. Apparently the eye is a small body, but in fact it is a great workshop, which accurately and regularly functions as a camera. It is a collection, which is compatible, aimed and connected and which follows a single aim and fullls an important need of man; that is to see objects. Truly, if there had been no sight, how dark this world would have been for us?!

Now we pose the following questions to our intellect and listen to its replies: Did the three layers of the eye appear on their own or it is someone else who had created them with foresight?

Did the transparent covering of the eye became transparent by chance or it is someone else who made them transparent so that light may pass through it?

How did the eye come to have transparent aqueous humor and vitreous body? Who has constructed these two liquids with special viscosity and formula? Were the glands that secrete these liquids aware of the needs of the eye? Did the pupil come into being automatically or it was the man who knew that the eye needed an aperture so that light may pass through it, and so he created it in this way?

Has the pupil itself selected the required diameter through foresight or it is someone else who has designed and created it in this way? Does the pupil know that it needs to be opened and shut to regulate the passage of light through it? Or it is someone else who informed it of this need and who created it in this way? Did the Yellow spot come to be located in line with the pupil and focus of the lens so that image may form on it or it is someone else who has placed it there?

Did the most sensitive cells of retina come to be situated exactly at the Yellow spot in line with lens or it is someone else who has placed them in this way? Do the optical nerves connect to the cells of yellow spot by chance so that their messages may be transferred to the brain or it is someone else who has preplanned this? Do the optical nerves connect the eye to the brain in aimless way by chance or they have an aim and a creator with aim who has done this?

Who has created the optical lens with such precision and which expert physicist has planned it?

Is the eye also aware of the science of physics and the discussion of lenses? Is the lens aware of its sensitive position? Is the covering of the lens automatically adjustable? Has the eye itself made the act of focusing possible for the lens or it is someone else who has determined this? And whether…?

Lastly, has this systematic, compatible and aimed device come into existence through chance and coincidence or it is a wise and a powerful creator who has created it? The reply is clear to all those who have sense: Study of intricate and diminutive machinery of our eye guides to its wise and powerful creator and in this intricate machinery, we ourselves see the signs of His knowledge and unending power.

Secondary Organs of the Machinery Of Sight

Here we shall learn about the rst of the secondary organs of the machinery of sight – without which the process of seeing remains defective. We would become familiar with it and after that through posing of questions we will seek to know who their creator is.

As mentioned before the machinery of sight consists of two parts: 1. The eyeball, which performs the function of seeing 2. Secondary organs, which are responsible for protecting the eye and ensuring its movement and hygiene. These organs are as follows: Eye socket, eyelids, tear glands, muscles surrounding the eyes and nerves. We shall explain each of them briey to know about their functions:

1. Eye socket: It is a bony hollow in the shape of a pyramid whose base is in the front and its tip is at the back. Eye socket is divided into two parts with a concave curtain: the front portion of which is the abode of the eyeball and the rear portion contains the optical nerves, muscles surrounding the eyeball, sensitive nerves and nerves of movement and blood veins; and the space between them is lled with fat tissue.
2. Eyebrows: Which are situated at the frontal portion of the eye socket and they prevent sweat from entering the eyes.
3. Eyelids: They are shaped as parts of skin which are stretched over the eyeball. Every eyelid has skin in its front surface portion and in its rear portion, muscles and tissues are attached to it. The inner surface of the eyelid is covered with a transparent tissue named conjunctiva. Muscles of the eyelid are of two types: 1. Muscles, which contract opening the eyelids 2. Circular muscles, which are pulled over the eyeball.

The function of the eyelids is to protect the eyeball and to prevent entry of foreign objects into it, especially during sleep when there is no need of the function of the eye; it covers its whole surface and protects it from possible dangers. Moreover, in the inner edge of the eyelids, holes are arranged and these (25 or 26 holes) secrete a special type of fat to soften the eyeball. The upper eyelid through systematic and swift movement coveys tears to every part of the eyeball and keep it moist and also does not allow any dust or dirt to accumulate in it.

1. Eyelashes: Which are is the form of some short strands of hair which grow from the edge of the eyelids.
2. Tear glands: Glands situated in the external upper portion of every eye are named as tear glands. These glands produce tears, which are composed of water and a little quantity of salt. Tears secreted from these glands keep the surface around the eyelids covering the eye always moist, and they wash it; the remaining tears collect in the inner corner of the eye and from there are sent to the nose through the tear duct where they gradually evaporate moistening the air which is inhaled.
3. Muscles surrounding the eye: These muscles of the eyeball cause it to move in different directions as follows:

A) Directly outward, which takes the eyeball outward.

B) Directly inward, which takes the eyeball inward and towards the nose. Contraction of directly outward muscles of each eye usually moves along with the muscles of the other eye as a result of which both eyes move to the right or the left in unison.

C) Directly upward muscles, which move the eyeball to the top.

D) Directly downward muscles, which move the eyeball down etc.

1. Nerves: These include the optical nerves, which receive optical messages from retina and transfer it to the center of brain in form of electrical impulses and other nerves.

A Discourse on Knowing God

Now we pose the following questions to ourselves: Is the eye aware of its importance and intricacy of its own existence that chose this solid eye socket as its abode? Or it was by chance that it came to occupy this safe place? Or it was someone else who provided this safe refuge to it as a result of foresight?

Did the eye itself brought into existence eyebrows above itself in order to prevent the entry of sweat? Or the eyebrow was aware of this need of the eye and it hastened to offer this help? Or it was someone else who created eyebrows above the eye?

Did the eyelids by chance become as such in order to protect and wash the eyes? Were the eyelids aware of the hygiene required by the eye that they rubbed fat over its surface and washed it through tears and continuous swift movement? Or it was a wise and a powerful creator who determined this?

Were the tear glands placed in the eye by chance? Who has devised the composition of this disinfectant liquid? Did the tear glands know that salty water is necessary to disinfect the surface of the eye? Is the hole in the corner of the eye – through which the excess tears are drained – come into existence by chance? Or it was the eye which procured this aperture? Was the eye aware of the need of the nose and the respiratory organs to moisten the inhaled air that it causes the excess tears to drain into the nose? Or it was a wise and a powerful creator who designed all this through foresight?

Do the holes that secrete fat in the eyelids come into being on their own? Or the eye, since it needed them, created them? Were the eyelids aware what help they are rendering to maintain the hygiene of the eye by secreting this fat?

Did the muscles of the eye and eyelids with those variations come into being of their own? Or did the eye bring them into existence? Or it was someone else who determined them on the basis of foresight?

Did the optical nerves with all their intricacy and specialty, connect the eye to the center of sight inside the brain automatically? Or it is a knowing being who has determined this connection?

In other words: Is such compatible and systematic collection, all parts of which are connected to each other and pursue and realize a single aim – that is to see – is it possible that it come into being on its own?

Yes, every intelligent person will reply that in such a compatible, interconnected and systematic collection – in whose make-up hundreds of laws and thousands of miniaturizations and amazements have come into action – it cannot be thought to have come into existence by chance or coincidence; it is the wise and a powerful creator who has brought them into existence.

This is the correct reply. When we look at the complex structure of the eyeball and when we study and contemplate on the connection of the eye to its secondary parts and the connection of all of them to the brain and the relationship of this collection with other parts of the body and the connection of the whole body to the outer world, we realize the whole world to be a single and great connection and witness that this great world is having a single, wise and powerful creator, who has created it and who also controls it.

If we look closely and with insight; we would be able to see the signs of the power, knowledge and wisdom of the great creator of the world everywhere. We shall recognize Him and connect ourselves to him with sincerity. And we would humble ourselves in front of His power and greatness and we would thank for the innumerable bounties and blessings from the depths of our hearts. His pure love would permeate throughout our selves. We would realize that only He is worthy of worship and we would accept only His commands and we would submit only to Him.

Circulatory System

The circulatory system is an extremely remarkable and amazing system of the human body. Even as you read this book, your heart beats approximately seventy times every minute and with continuous and precise beats conveys nourishment and oxygen to all the cells of your body. Do you know what would happen if your heart stops beating only for a few minutes?

Study of our circulatory system (heart, veins, arteries and capillary hair...) guides us to the existence of a wise and a powerful creator.

Blood ows at the edge of and around all the cells of the body like a steam of water and it conveys nourishment and oxygen to them. Red globules oat in the liquid of blood. In every cubic millimeter of blood, there are approximately ve million red globules and in the body of every man there are around 25000 million red globules. These globules have a very intricate and remarkable function.

Their function is to convey oxygen to the cells and to recover carbon dioxide from them and in order to fulll this life-giving function they to moving and circulating through the body nerves continuously. The length of this passage is great. An average red globule has the life-span of 120 days and new globules are being continuously manufactured by the blood making center of the body.

It would be better if we organize a scienic journey with a group of globules so that we may understand the various stages of this journey and we may be able to look closely at the intricate and amazing system of blood circulation. Denitely by seeing this systematic and amazing compatibility we would say: Great, wise and powerful is the creator, who has created such an elaborate system.

First Stage

If you have a photo or a picture in your house; you should look at it, look at the left vertical of the heart. Our supposed journey begins at 9 am on Saturday in the company of a group of red globules, which are carrying oxygen with them. The contraction of the left ventricle creates a severe movement, which takes us to the outer stage. It is extremely amazing and interesting that we have reached into a wide and a branched canal, the aorta, which has many branches, distributes blood and conveys to every organ a xed amount of blood.

Passage

Through continuous and repeated beatings, which reach us from the rear we are in such motion; and we ask the globules with whom we are traveling: What is our route and where are we headed? They reply: We are moving to the brain. Continuous contractions of the heart create new beats and send us forward; the passage gradually becomes narrow and narrower, so narrow that if it is almost a hundredth of a human hair; these are known as capillaries and they are extremely thin and have many loops.

Stage of Narrow Passages

We ask our co-traveler globules: Shall we rest for a while enroute? They reply: No, but at the edge of these cells we would reduce our speed and give them the oxygen that we are carrying and take carbon dioxide from them, which is the byproduct of the heating of the cells and take it back with us. Here we saw that the oxygen that the globules carry is given to the cells and the cells take up the freshly inhaled oxygen and give back carbon dioxide to the globules.

Moreover, we also saw that the cells secrete their excess matter into the blood stream so that the blood may take it away from there to be disposed at another place.

Return Journey

The color and form of the red globules have changed and it is no more having that same joy and happiness and passing through other narrow and interlaced passages with which they are well acquainted; they are on the return journey. Where are they returning? To the heart on the return route they are being beaten continuously from the rear through the contractions of the heart and we are being pushed ahead as if something is pulling us ahead. Gradually the way widens and we pass through the aorta and reach a dark passage and ask what its name is. It replies: Artery (as impure blood passes through it) and nally we reach the end of our journey into the heart.

Entering the Right Atrium

Now that we have reached the heart, has our journey come to an end? No…on the contrary we rest only for a short while and the valve below us opens and all of us enter the right ventricle. It is explained that this ventricle is having three parts and its function is extremely sensitive. It operates only on one side and it opens only from the atrium into the ventricle and it does not open from the ventricle into the atrium. On the contrary it closes completely and without leaving any hole or gap for the blood to ow into the ventricle.

Severe Beating

At the stage of the three-lobed ventricle, we feel that we have been given a hard push and thrown out of the right ventricle. Where are we going? To the lungs. What for? To obtain oxygen. Through some continuous beatings, we reach to the alveoli. Globules are present at the edge of free air, which enters the lungs from outside. In the lungs, oxygen is picked up and carbon dioxide eliminated, and the oxygenated blood returns to the heart via the pulmonary veins, thus completing the circuit.

Entering the Left Atrium

After the globules take up oxygen they enter the atrium happily and the valve (mitral valve) opens downwards and goes into its rst stage in the left ventricle as before. We immediately bids farewell to it before a powerful contraction could send us back to that same channel and thus we separate from our friends.

In this supposed journey we come to know about two types of blood circulations: General circulation and pulmonary circulation. General blood circulation begins from the left ventricle of the heart like a powerful pump and sends the blood to all the tissues of the body and ends at the right ventricle. Pulmonary circulation begins from the right ventricle and passing through capillaries reaches the lungs and after the exchange of oxygen and carbon dioxide, returns to the left ventricle.

Stages of Heartbeat

After a compatible and simultaneous contractions of the ventricles, the atriums open and pull the blood from the arteries to themselves and gradually ll up. At this point begins the general expansion of the heart as at this stage all the cavities of the heart are at rest:

1. Contraction of the atrium takes place after the general restfulness and sends the two bloods from the atriums to the ventricles.
2. Contraction of the ventricles, which on one hand send blood to body tissues and on the other hand send it to the lungs.
3. General rest

These three stages together occur in approximately one-eighth of a second and in this way the heart of a human being beats for 70 times a minute.

A Discourse on Knowing God

If we look at the intricate and systematic working of the heart and blood circulation, we would realize that this advanced and remarkable machinery is having a wise and a powerful creator who has created it with this minuteness and nesse.

To further motivate reection we can pose the following questions to our intellects and seek replies to them:

1. With all this complexity and marvel, is it possible that the heart came into being on its own without any aim?
2. Do the atriums and ventricles of the heart themselves assumed their present shapes and forms?
3. Did the heart valves plan such a responsibility and specialty for themselves and then brought themselves into existence?
4. Has the elegant network of veins, capillaries and capillary hairs come into being automatically and by coincidence?
5. Has discipline, compatibility and cooperation between the heart and network of veins and respiratory system developed through chance? Or whether…?

Your intelligent reply is absolutely clear: A great, wise and powerful creator has created such an amazing system. God is great.

A Glance at the Created World

In the morning you see how the sun rises gently from behind the mountains and what beauty it carries and how it illuminates the plains and elds. Truly what beauty and clarity this illuminated ball bestows to the mountains and plains! Just think! If the sun does not arise and all the time it is only a dark night what we would have done? Have you thought how the sun got such light and heat? Do you know how much is the volume of the sun?

The volume of the sun is approximately a million times that of the earth. That is if the sun was a ball empty from inside, it would have accommodated nearly one million earths inside it. The surface temperature of this ery ball is 6000 degrees centigrade. You know that with all this heat how it heats up this earth and all that is on it. Since it is situated at an appropriate and determined distance (at a distance of around 150 million kilometers) it conveys only necessary light and elements to the earth.

No one knows what would have happened if the distance of the sun to the earth had not been as such. If the distance of the sun to the earth had been less than this; for example it had been half of this, what would have happened? It is denite that no living being would have been able to survive on its surface, and the heat of the sun would have scorched all the plants, animals and human beings. If the distance of the sun to the earth had been more than this; for example if it had been twice than what it is at present, what would have happened?

In that case, sufcient light and heat would not have reached the earth and everything would have frozen to death. All the water would have frozen to ice and no life would have survived. Thus it is clear that this distance is linked to an awareness, precision, determination and foresight.

It is through the light and heat of the sun that pretty bunches of wheat reach such ripeness; it is as a result of the hot rays of the sun that all vegetation and trees reach maturity and provide fruits and food for us human beings. Different types of foods that we obtain are prepared through the energy of the sun. It is in fact the energy of the sun, which collects in all plants and food articles and we gain energy from them. Animals also benet from the energy stored in plants and they transfer them to us in form of animal food. For example, they feed on grass and provide us with milk and we also benet from the meat and other secondary foods based on milk and meat.

What do you understand by contemplating on the glory and beauty of the sun, its precise and determined distance to the earth, benet of the plants, animals and human beings from the heat and energy of the sun? And what do you conclude after seeing and pondering on the perpetuity and amazing compatibility of all the parts of the world? What do you see? Do you see an unsystematic and incompatible collection or a collection which is great and perfectly compatible; of which we are also a part. What can you conclude from the system and compatibility of this precise collection?

System and precision, which encompasses all the parts of this world, what does it show? Can you reply to this query in a foolish way and say: The creator of this great system is a being who is unaware, ignorant and powerless? Such a reply would never be accepted by our awakened conscience and wise intellect. On the contrary it would say: The intricate system and the coherence and perpetuity of this great collection is a sign of the greatness, power and awareness of a superior creator who is capable of creating and controlling the beings of this world in this way and he had the foresight to know from before the needs of each of them perfectly and gave them the capacity to fulll them. He also determined the path and aim for each of them. Who is that powerful and knowing creator?

That knowing and powerful creator is none but God, who has created all the bounties for us and which He has given under our control. He created the sun, moon and earth for us so that we might through efforts and cooperation, inhabit the earth and by obtaining knowledge and learning, discover the secrets and amazements and look at the great signs of our creator and Lord and through condential prayers beseech Him:

The highest and the best condition of man is when he supplicates his Lord and beseeches Him in secret. And if supplication and secret prayer to his God had not been there, what value life would have had? How worthless man would have been?

You contemplate on the creation of the night and day and every morning and evening you recite condential supplications to the creator of the night and day. You know that night and day is due to rotation of the earth. Every night and day completes one rotation. Half the earth which comes before the sun is illuminated and it is day over there and the other half is dark and it is night over there. By rotation of the earth, the day seems to be entering the night and the night seems to be entering the day and days and nights follow each other in a systematic way. During the day, plants and trees grow under the light and heat of the sun. Human beings become involved in efforts and work renovated by the rest they got during the night and begin a new day with more vigor and supplication to the Almighty.

Have you ever thought what would have happened if the rotation of the earth had not been so systematic and precise? In some parts of the earth there would have been perpetual nights and in some parts there would have been continuous day; hot and scorching. Appearance of day and night are also clear signs of the power, greatness and awareness of the wise and powerful creator of the world.

Three Important Points

1. We should look in the world of creation, and ponder and realize the system, coherence and compatibility of its innumerable parts and ask: "Who has created this world and who controls it?"
2. The great and systematic collection of the world of creation is clear evidence that: "A knowing and powerful creator has created it and only He controls it, and He is God."
3. The knowing and powerful God who has created the world has also determined duties for our growth and success; the most important of which may be listed as follows:
4. We look at the signs of the greatness and power of our Lord and contemplate on it.
5. That we discover the secrets and amazing aspects of the world through knowledge and learning.
6. That we gain proximity to Him through worship and supplications.
7. That we inhabit the earth through efforts and cooperation and spread justice and equity in it.

Every Phenomenon has a cause

You move your hand and pick up the pen, but your friend does not move his hand and pick up the pen, why? It is so because you intended to pick up the pen your friend had no such intention and desire. The intention of picking up the pen is a new phenomenon which is actualized in yourself; you have brought this new phenomenon into existence. Intention is related to you and is the act of yourself, and the movement of the hand is also related to you and is your intention. You did not move your hand previously since you had no intention; you intended at a later stage and after intending, you moved your hand and picked up the pen. The phenomenon of intention is the effect of you; if you had not been there, no intention would have taken place. The intention has not come into being on its own; on the contrary it is from you. There is a special relationship between you and intention, which is called as the relationship of cause and effect. You see this special relationship in your own being with perfect clarity and are perfectly aware of it.

Another Example

You have the memory of a bunch of owers that you had previously seen; now you recall it (which is called as the imaginative form): This image of the owers is a new phenomenon, which has come in your mind. Has it appeared automatically or you have brought it into being? Of course, you have brought it into existence. If you were not there, the form of the owery branch would also not have been there.

This mental image is related to you; that is its existence is not independent; on the contrary it has come into existence from you. You are the cause and the mental image is the effect and this special relationship is named as the relationship of the cause and effect. You see this relationship in your own self and are perfectly familiar with it.

Therefore, we conclude that you and every person will nd the causality in the self and you see it perfectly clearly.

Moreover, you will nd this special relationship, 'relationship of the cause and effect' between yourself and your bodily and mental acts and relate them to yourself as you are their cause and say: I saw, I heard, I touched, I smelt, I tasted, I moved, I thought…you consider yourself as the cause and seeing, hearing, touching, smelling, tasting, moving and thinking as you effects and connected to you. These actions have originated from your being and if you had not been there, your actions and movements would also not have been there.

Man has named causation that is the relationship with the cause to effect as the law of cause and effect. In the beginning between his own being and spiritual and mental phenomena and verbalized his movements and actions between his own self and his mental phenomena, actions and movements; then he transmitted this law from outside his being.

Law Of Causation Is A Fundamental, Absolute And Universal Law

Man, on the basis of that realization when he comes across a phenomenon whose existence depends on (or is related to) another phenomenon he understands that between these two phenomena also the relationship of cause and effect is present and in these circumstances he decides that the phenomena which are themselves in need of others are effects and the factor which has brought these into existence is the cause.

Man through study, research and excessive experiments has concluded that some worldly phenomenon have different types of relationships with other phenomena; such relationship which exist between himself and his mental phenomena and on the basis of this deep understanding he accepts the law of causation to be complete and universal.

It is like completing a job in anticipation of its desired result; it is the best evidence that one has accepted the law of causality as a comprehensive law, on drinking water he awaits for the quenching of thirst and on eating, waits for the satiation of his hunger. In winter, he takes the refuge of warmth of re and in summer heat he looks for the coolness of shade. In any case, all of us in daily life and in all our movements and actions accept causality as an absolute and universal fundamental and in this way create an impression.

No Effect Is Without Cause

If the window opens and you have not seen who opened it, what will you think? Would you say that it opened automatically (without any cause)? If you heard a sound and do not see what has produced it, what will you conclude? Would you think that it came by coincidence and without any proper cause? If you heard a voice and do not see who has produced it, what will you conclude? If you feel hot or cold, would you think that it has no cause? If a stone is thrown at the window, breaking the glass and you cannot nd who has thrown it, what would you conclude? Would you conclude that the stone arose from the ground automatically and without any cause and hit the glass?

Your reply to the above questions is clear. You will say: I possess reason and intellect and I know that none of the worldly phenomena are without a cause or a doer, even though I might not know what the cause is, because not knowing it is not the proof of its absence. That is why you will make as much investigation and be curious about it till you don't nd the real cause of the phenomena. And if suppose you cannot nd the cause in one instance, you will not say that it has no cause, on the contrary you would say that the cause of this phenomenon is not known.

Intellectuals and inventors have fully accepted the law of causation and they try to nd the cause of things in laboratories. Whenever they come across a new phenomenon, they are certain that it is having a cause and that is why they conduct fresh efforts to nd it.

World Is Also Having A Cause

We know that the law of cause and effect is a fundamental, absolute and a universal law. And no phenomenon is without a cause and all the phenomena of the world have a cause. This complete law is practically accepted by everyone in the world.

Every phenomenon has a cause, if the cause of that is a phenomenon it also has a cause, therefore since the whole created world is a phenomenon and needful and does not have independent existence – it is in need of someone or something superior; basically being in need of another is the rst quality of a phenomenon, every big and small phenomenon is – needful and related to someone or something else, its existence is not on its own, if it had existed independently, it would have endured forever and had also not been needful. The world of phenomena is needful of existence and being, that is why it is in need of a being that is higher and needful – which is the source of bestowing existence to all the phenomena and the existing beings are needful and limited.

That being which is higher and that incomparable and unlimited entity, which is the source of existence and which does not have any defect and need, is the Almighty God. He is the one who created this world, is always controlling it through his blessings and nurtures it. If His blessing and favor is cut off for even a moment, all would be destroyed.

Objection

You said that every phenomenon is in need of a cause; therefore God also is in need of a cause, what is the cause of God? In other words: God has created every existing thing, so who has created God?

Reply

Yes, we said that every phenomenon is needful of a cause, but I did not say that every entity is needful of a cause; therefore every phenomenon and every existing thing, which is needful and limited, is in need of a cause, but not the Almighty Allah who is Self-sufcient and a perfect entity. He does not have need of a cause. Existence is His very being. He does not have any need that others may fulll His need.

In other words, the criteria of needfulness of cause is need and limitation; and generosity and personal poverty; and there is no defect and limitation in God Almighty that He should have need of cause; on the contrary he is absolutely Self-sufcient and there is nothing higher than Him that He should be need of it; if he had been the effect of another, He would have been in need of that other and in that case he would not be God. He is there by Himself and by His own being and others endure because of Him; God is higher and superior.

In the Holy Quran, He says:

> "O men! you are they who stand in need of Allah, and Allah is He Who is the Self-sufcient, the Praised One." (35:15)

Explanation of Reasoning About Knowing God

Man is intelligent and he is having foresight. He can understand the realities of the world through contemplation and making logical reasonings. So far we have learnt about two reasonings of Knowing God: proof of order and proof of causation. We have also discussed these two topics in some details:

With regard to the reasoning of order, we said: The created world is based on order, system and coordination and perfect relationship; every order, system and coordination and determination is created by a wise and powerful creator; thus this world is also the creation of a wise and a powerful creator.

In this reasoning (reasoning of order) we rst pay attention to the order, coordination, precision and determination that is present between parts of the world and at that time with reference to this belief that 'every system and determination has an aware and a powerful coordinator and determiner', we conclude that this great order and coordination in this world also has a wise and a powerful creator.

But in the evidence of cause, we don't see other than order and compatibility between the phenomena of this world; on the contrary, we looked at the being and the existence of phenomena and noted the need and special need which every phenomenon has for cause – that every person has profound belief in it – we present the matter in this manner:

Every phenomenon that comes into existence, its existence is not independent; on the contrary it is related and dependant on something else, which is called as the cause.

This world is also composed of various phenomena; therefore it has to have a cause.

With regard to the reasoning of causality it can be said that every phenomenon that comes into being, its existence is dependant and needful. And its being is not on its own, on the contrary it is dependent on a cause and the world and everything present in it on one side is a phenomenon and all are created – so they must have come into being from the source of creation and we call that unlimited power as God.

Both the reasonings of order and causality are to remove the dust of ignorance and carelessness from the eyes of foresight and nature of man, so that he may see the reality with a clean nature and an awakened intellect. And that he sees the brightest of the bright and strengthens his faith in the High and the Mighty Lord.

But the pure natures of man are aware of his great and powerful creator in such a way and this matter is so clear to them that they require the least reasonings. These pure natures and aware persons consider everything to be relying on the power and invincible determination of Almighty Allah and in all hardships and difculties, he takes refuge in Him and is never aficted with despair and hopelessness, since he knows no matter how powerful the phenomena may be they are in need of Almighty God and they are under His control. These pure natures and these aware persons – since they saw that everything was in need of God – they do not submit to anything other than the Almighty Allah and they do not accept any command and guardianship except His – and join the life of the world with respect and success with everlasting happiness of the hereafter.

Ultimately, we consider it necessary to mention that in order to prove the existence of the creator of the world we also depend on evidences in books of philosophy and scholasticism for numerous and profound reasonings; but for the sake of brevity, we shall be content with this much.

It is mentioned in the Holy Quran:

"...your Lord is the Lord of the heavens and the earth, Who brought them into existence..." **(21:56)**

Qualities of God

On the basis of the discussion so far, we have understood that this world is having a cause which has created and manages it. In this section, we would learn about the qualities of Almighty God, in order to recognize Him better. The qualities of God can be divided into two: Qualities of perfection and qualities of majesty.

Every quality that is from perfections and elevated ranks is the root of existence and which increases its value and existence. Without that it should necessitate defect and limitation, is named as the quality of perfection and beauty. Like: knowledge, power, life, hearing, sight, intention, speaking, benecence, mercy and other such qualities.

For example knowledge, which can be dened as the presence, appearance and existence of a thing for the knower, is a perfection of existence. And there is no defect in its meaning and its evidence is not described as one necessitating defect and limitation.

Although it is possible that it may be true in some limited implications, but this implication has not appeared from the aspect of defect and limitation, on the contrary it is a rank from the ranks of existence and which comes into existence from the root. And in this way the quality of power and life is also included as the qualities of perfection.

The Almighty Allah is the possessor of all of them and is endowed with them. Qualities of perfection are also called as Positive Attributes (Sifaat-e-Thubutiyyah), as they are proved to belong to Allah.

Scholars have mentioned reasonings to prove the qualities of perfection for Almighty Allah and two of those reasonings are comparatively simple:

First evidence – These perfections exist outwardly, knowledge is in the outward and some existing beings possess knowledge, power also exists outwardly and some existing beings possess power and perform some actions. Life is also in the outward and some existing beings are alive and perform their functions with knowledge and intention.

Thus the qualities of perfection have an outward existence and are themselves a phenomenon and as we stated previously, every phenomenon is in need of a cause and a doer that invents it, and that is the Almighty Allah, the creator of the world. Therefore since existent beings and phenomena of the world in fact are related to the being of the Almighty Allah, the qualities of being and perfection are also related to God and it is Him that has bestowed those qualities to them. On the other hand, the Bestower of perfection Himself possesses those perfections. On the contrary He is higher than those stages. God, who has given knowledge, power and life to the creatures, it is not possible for Him to lack those qualities. If He did not have them, He would not have been able to bestow others with them.

Second evidence is the proof of order – You discovered and understood the various aspects of the precise and amazing system by the creator of the world in the previous lessons, that how much precision and beauties He has employed in their creation and with what connection and precise coordination has

He created and managed them although all phenomena of the beautiful world are inter-related. Through study of such an amazing and compatible system it can be easily concluded that their creator is also is all-knowing, powerful and living, and he has created this precise system through knowledge, power and plan and He has been aware and aimed in its creation.

Existence of such a precise and beautiful system is the best proof that their creator has knowledge, power and life. But can senseless matter create and manage such a precise and coordinated system? Or can a book of science or a beautiful work of art be produced from a senseless and weak being? Then how can it be imagined that this great world, with all the secrets and amazing things, with such system and coordination could have come into being from senseless and non-intentional nature?

Attributes of Perfection

In the previous lessons, where the process and relationship of cause and effect was explained and proved, it became clear that: the effect no matter how much perfection and beauty it had, all of it is received from its cause and the cause is in possession of all these perfections and beauty at a higher scale. Therefore God Almighty, who is the creator and real cause of the heavens and earth and all that is present in them, He possesses all the perfections and beauties of the universe.

Knowledge, power and life are the attributes of perfection, which are present in some creatures: sight, hearing and speech are the attributes of perfection, which man is in possession of.

We consider the learned and aware man due to his learning and awareness to be superior and more perfect than one who is not in possession of this knowledge. We also consider the powerful and strong man due to his power and strength to be superior to one who does not have this power and strength. The seeing and the hearing man or one who has these two qualities is in possession of perfections, which a blind and deaf person does not have.

Therefore we say: Life, knowledge, power, insight are the attributes of perfection and values that some creatures possess them in a limited quantum. For example, the body of man possesses life, but this life is limited in every aspect; if he does not eat, he would die; if he does not breathe, he would die. His life has a beginning and an end; it has limitations and conditions.

Man is seeing, but his sight is limited and conditional, and he cannot see beyond a distance and he cannot see the whole world in a single moment. He is also unable to see in the dark…and in this way every attribute of perfection present in the creatures is limited and conditional.

Seeing the perfections and beauties present in existing things we conclude that the God of the world, is the creator and the real creator cause of all creatures, and He possesses these attributes; because if He had not possessed them, He would not have been able to bestow them to the creatures. But the perfections that the Almighty Allah possesses do not have any condition and limitation and they do not

have any decrease and are much higher.

Since we conclude that God is the possessor of all perfections that exist in the world, we describe the Almighty Allah with these qualities and say: God is living. God is all-knowing. God is all-powerful. God is seeing. God is hearing. God is speaking. God is merciful. God is benecent, God is self- sufcient…but since all of us are concerned in a limited and restricted sense with these qualities, we use comparison in our descriptions and we say: God is living, but not like our life which is limited, decient and which is to end, on the contrary He is much higher.

God is knowing, but not like our knowledge, which is limited and decient and which can be separated from our being, that sometimes we are knowing and sometimes ignorant; therefore we always accompany our description with two sentences: 'Allah is the greatest' and 'Glory be to Allah' as both these sentences absolve the Almighty Allah of every kind of limitation, defect and shortcoming.

Can we imagine God and His Attributes?

This imagination implies whether we can see God and His attributes in our imagination? It is clear that we can imagine the scenes of the heavens and we can imagine the scene of sunset. We can imagine the face of parents and affection of parents. Can we imagine God and His attributes in the same way? If we see what we imagine, we would see that it is also limited and it has occupied our imagination. But that which is unlimited in every way, cannot be occupied in a limited mind. Therefore when we imagine the attributes of the perfection of Allah and for example, when we think about His power, we should say: Allah is the greatest and glory be to God; that is Allah is the most superior and is pure of every defect and deciency.

Comparison: How will you describe the sea to one who has never seen it?

Just suppose one of your friends has never seen the sea; how will you describe it to him? You would have to help his intelligence and imagination. For example if he has seen a small pond or a small ditch lled with rain water, you will say: sea is also a water body, but not like these water bodies, on the contrary it is much bigger and deeper; you would say: sea is also a pool of water like these pools, but much deeper, wider, but in spite of that some of those who have never seen the sea would not be able to imagine its wideness and depth and you will have to say that the sea is much wider and deeper than what you imagine.

Somewhat such is our condition with regard to the attributes of perfection of God; in every perfection we see a small pool having hundreds of limits, restrictions and defects; but we understand that Almighty Allah is having all these perfections and beauties in an unbounded and limitless manner and without any defect or shortcoming; therefore with imagination of every quality of perfection that we see in the creatures, we remove limit and restrictions from it and associate it to Allah and as much good the quality is, we believe in its better and higher form for the Almighty Allah and although the Almighty Allah is much

higher than the description of one who does not recognize Him. (Glory be to God from what they attribute to Him except the sincere servants of Allah)

Can God be Seen?

Eyes can see things, for example that tree which is in the garden of the school and that ower which grows under the tree will also be seen with the eye. Our eyes can see only some bodies among all the existing beings. Bodies which are in range of sight and sufcient light from them reaches to the eyes are only the ones visible to the eyes.

But the eyes are not able to see many things which are at a great distance or lie beyond the focus of the eyes. Can the eyes see all that which lies in the depths of the skies and seas? Moreover, there are many things which are present, but which are not visible to the human eye; for example, you possess knowledge, intellect and love; are they visible to your eyes; or it is that their effects are seen by the eyes.

If we had been able to see God with the eyes, He would indeed have had a body like other bodies and which occupy a space and which are present at one place and absent elsewhere, He would have been like a creature, like other creatures which are limited and which need space; and like other things which have a beginning and an end, and which go on changing from one state to another. If God had been a body, He would be present here and absent there. And He could not have been able to create and see the things which are there. If God had been a body like other bodies of creatures He would not have been their creator and superior to them. That is why since God is not a body He cannot be seen with the physical eyes, on the contrary He can be discovered by reason and insight of man through seeing existing things (which are in fact His signs and effects). Eyes cannot see Him but He sees all eyes and He is most knowing and is well informed in every aspect.

Some Attributes Of Perfection

1. **Power:** God is powerful; that is He can do anything that is logically possible. He performs all His acts from the aspect of knowledge, choice and intention and He is neither compelled to do anything or to leave it. His power is endless and without any limit. In the Holy Quran, He says:

   "..surely Allah has power over all things." (2:20)

1. **Knowledge:** That is He knows everything and encompasses all existing things and worldly phenomena; and nothing is hidden from Him; so much so that He is also cognizant of the intentions and thoughts of people. He says in Quran:

   "Say: Whether you hide what is in your hearts or manifest it, Allah knows it, and He knows whatever is in the heavens and whatever is in the earth, and Allah has power over all things." (3:29)

1. **Life:** God is living. That is He is a being that acts according to knowledge and power. Life of God does not imply that He breathes and moves like human beings and that he eats and grows. On the contrary, it implies that His acts are based on intention and knowledge.
2. **Intention:** God is having intention; that is He performs His actions with intention. And He is not like re, which had no intention of its own to burn and which does not have discretion.

But He does whatever He wants. And if He does not make an intention, He does not do it. His intention and will is a perfection of the subject but God who is at the ultimate stage of perfection and existence, would not lack any of these perfections. In Quran also, intention is related to God. He says:

"Our word for a thing when We intend it, is only that We say to it, Be, and it is." (16:40)

And He says:

"Surely Allah will cause those who believe and do good deeds to enter gardens beneath which rivers ow, surely Allah does what He pleases." (22:14)

1. **Hearing:** God is hearing; that is He is aware of every sound and nothing is hidden from Him.
2. **Seeing:** God is seeing. That is He can see every event and phenomenon and He is the witness and seer of them all. In Quran also, in numerous places, hearing and seeing is related to God. For example the Almighty Allah says:

"Surely Allah commands you to make over trusts to their owners and that when you judge between people you judge with justice; surely Allah admonishes you with what is excellent; surely Allah is Seeing, Hearing." (4:58)

1. **Speech:** God is speaking. That is He can express and explain His facts and aims to others...these are some of the qualities of perfection or positive attributes with which the Almighty Allah is described.

He possesses other attributes and names also, which are presently not mentioned here.

Important Reminder

Qualities of God are not decient and limited like our qualities. Since we are decient in attributes and being, we cannot do anything without senses and physical organs. Although we possess them, we cannot do anything without seeking limbs and organs. We possess the capacity to hear but we cannot hear without ears. We possess the capacity to see but we cannot hear without eyes.

But the being of the Almighty Allah, since it is at the ultimate level of perfection and His qualities also are perfected to the highest level, He sees without eyes, He hears without ears and performs acts without limbs and organs and He understands without brain and nerves. Since the way of seeing and hearing is that they can only be performed through eyes, ears and nerves, on the contrary the reality of seeing and hearing is nothing except that they should be for a person who is apparent and clear, although it should be without the interference of senses.

We also, if we had not been defective, would have been able to see and hear without the interference of eyes and ears; indeed seeing and hearing would have been proved from them. But the Lord of the created world, since with regard to His being and qualities is at the ultimate level of perfection, His qualities and acts are also perfect and unrestricted and do not have needs like us.

In the same way, since we are decient, we are compelled to use the tongue, mouth and outlets of pronunciation in explaining our aims, but Almighty Allah has no need of tongue and mouth in speaking and expressing Himself, but He expresses His aims in other ways and which is also speaking. Since speaking does not only mean that its aims should be expressed through the tongue and mouth, on the contrary if this same action can be performed without tongue and mouth, it would also be considered speaking.

Therefore the qualities of God are very much different from our qualities.

Negative Attributes

Every attribute that negates defect and limitation for the Almighty Allah is called as negative attribute. It is also called as Sifat Salbiya, because their meaning is negative. The being of the Almighty Allah is a perfect being without any limit and is having no defect and limitation. That is why He is having necessity of existence and absence cannot be imagined about Him. He possesses all perfections and no perfection can be taken away from Him.

On the contrary, He is pure of every kind of defect. Qualities that negate His defects are called as Negative attributes or Sifaat Salbiyah. They are too many, but here we mention only a few of them:

1) God is not Body: Body is something which possesses length and breath, depth and form, which occupies space according to its volume and it cannot remain without having a special space. And that is why God is not a body, because if He had been a body He would need space, so that He may occupy it. And such a needful being cannot be Necessary Being (Wajibul Wujud), because necessity of being is not compatible with needfulness and limitation. God is the creator of spaces, how can He be needful of space?

2) God is not visible to Physical Eyes: That is He cannot be seen with material eyes, because only bodies, effects and their specialties can be seen with eyes, while the fact is that we have proved above that God is not a body. Therefore He would never be visible. Almighty Allah would neither be seen in this world nor in the world of the hereafter.

He is an unlimited and abstract being without the effects and qualities of matter and body; how can He become visible to a material eye? Eyes can see a thing which is placed at a particular distance from it.

Since the being of God is neither limited nor occupies space, in that case it is possible that someone says: If God had existed He would have been visible to the eye or perceived through one of the senses. How can His being be accepted when none of the senses perceive Him? It would be said in reply: The scope of being is not conned to perceptions; in this world we are having hundreds and thousands of material things, which cannot be perceived through senses.

Can you not see the power of gravity of the earth and power of electricity in wires? Can you see electrons and protons present in an atom and their movement? Can you see life in a living thing? Can you see the human and animal soul? Can you see the affection of the mother for her children? Can you see and hear all the sounds in the atmosphere? Etc.

Even though all these things are material and physical, they are not perceived by any of the senses, but you accept their existence, since you see their effects.

Thus how can you expect to see the creator of the world when He is a being abstract of matter and materiality and much above time and space? Such unlimited being cannot occupy the limited vessel of perception, but you see the effects and signs of the creator of the world in the beauties and amazing aspects of the world and gain faith in His being.

In the Holy Quran also, it is mentioned clearly that the Almighty Allah would never be visible to the physical eyes:

"Vision comprehends Him not, and He comprehends (all) vision; and He is the Knower of subtleties, the Aware." (6:103)

3) God is not Ignorant: In the discussion of Positive Attributes it was proved that knowledge is a perfection of being which the holy being of God possesses. Since the being of God is unlimited, His knowledge would also be unlimited and He is aware of everything in every condition and defect and ignorance is not present in His being. Therefore the Almighty Allah is not ignorant.

It is mentioned in the Holy Quran:

> *"Allah – surely nothing is hidden from Him in the earth or in the heaven." (3:5)*

4) God is not Helpless: Previously in the discussion of the Positive attributes, we proved that power is an excellence and the being of God is in possession of it. And since the Almighty Allah is an unlimited being, His power is also not having any limit, and He has power over every possible matter. That is why God is not helpless in anything.

5) He is not subject to Change: He does not age and is not susceptible to disease. He neither sleeps nor gets tired. He does not become regretful of consequences, because such qualities are only associated with materiality and physicality; and since we have already proved that God is not a physical body, such changes can never apply to Him. Therefore knowledge, hearing and seeing, intention and His other positive attributes are also such that they cannot change or be affected by anything.

It is said in the Holy Quran:

> *"Allah is He besides Whom there is no god, the Ever living, the Self-subsisting by Whom all subsist; slumber does not overtake Him nor sleep..." (2:255)*

6) God does not occupy Space: He can neither be conned to a place either in the earth or the heavens, because He is not a body that He should be in need of space. He is the creator of the spaces and He existed before them. God is a being abstract from matter and materiality and He encompasses all the beings and He does not occupy a particular vessel. His being is unlimited and unrestricted and He encompasses all the places. He is present and seeing everywhere and the terms of 'here' and 'there' are not used about Him.

But when we raise our hands to the sky in supplication it does not imply that we consider God to be in the heavens. On the contrary we express our humility and sincerity to Him and we visualize ourselves as a helpless and an anxious beggar.

Also if we label a mosque and the Kaaba as the House of Allah, it is so because we mean to say that the Almighty Allah is worshipped in them and that He had Himself honored them by mentioning them as His houses.

7) Allah is not Needful: Allah is a being that is unlimited and perfect from every aspect and no defect, limit or absence is present in His being. That is why He is a Necessary Being (Wajibul Wujud) and absence and deciency cannot be imagined about Him. And since He is such, He is not in need of anything. All perfections are bestowed by Him and He Himself in the position of a unique being is in possession of all perfections. He does not lack anything that he should be in need of it. Therefore God is not needful of anyone or anything.

If He has xed duties for the people and wants them to struggle in Jihad, it is not because He is in need of worship and Jihad. On the contrary, people themselves are in need of religion, Jihad and worship for perfection of selves and success of hereafter. And merciful God by sending the prophets and framing of laws and rules of religion has guaranteed their needs. People do not favor God by being religious, on the contrary the Almighty Allah is Kind that He has favored and guided them by sending prophets and framing laws for them.

If He has made Zakat and Khums obligatory, and asked people to help the needy and use funds in charitable and public welfare, it is not because He is in need of material help of the people; it is because such things are necessary to administer society and are there for the well-being of the people in general.

Moreover, the Almighty Allah favored human beings and the material help, which was for the well-being of human society, He labeled it as worship act. On the contrary He considered it to be the greatest worship act. Such that if it is performed with the intention of solely seeking the proximity of God, it will be a factor of perfection of self and will earn a hundred fold reward in the world of the hereafter.

8) God is not Unjust: God never commits any kind of injustice since He does not require anything that He should be unjust. More details on this matter will be mentioned in the discussion of divine justice.

9) God has no Partner: Neither has He a partner in creation nor in the administration of the world; nor has He permitted taking anyone or anything else as a deity. More details on this matter will be mentioned in the discussion of oneness of God.

It is mentioned in the Holy Quran:

> *"Surely Allah does not do injustice to the weight of an atom, and if it is a good deed He multiplies it and gives from Himself a great reward." (4:40)*

Oneness of God

Oneness of the godhead is the fundamental principle of all heavenly religions and a specialty of the religion of Islam. Divine prophets called people to belief in oneness of God and monotheism and prohibited them from polytheism and duality. The Holy Prophet of Islam (S) began his mission with monotheism and in the rst stage announced: Say 'there is no god except Allah' and be successful. Laws and beliefs of Islam are based on the oneness of the godhead.

The Holy Quran has accorded a special position to monotheism through numerous verses in such a way that it can be said to be a book of monotheism that opposes polytheism. The Holy Quran considers polytheism to be the only sin which is unforgivable under every circumstance. And He says:

> *"Surely Allah does not forgive that anything should be associated with Him, and forgives what is besides that to whomsoever He pleases..." (4:48)*

There are many kinds of monotheisms and we mention some of them in brief as follows:

Monotheism of the Being

Monotheism of the being implies that all worldly phenomena are caused by a single being and except Him there is no other creator. The great being, who is called as 'Allah' is one and not more and He is unique. He has an independent existence without any need whereas all phenomena of the world are related to Him and are in need of Him.

"Say: He, Allah, is One." (112:1)

And He says:

"Say: He is only one God, and surely I am clear of that which you set up (with Him)." (6:19)

In books of philosophy and scholasticism oneness of the godhood is proved through various logical reasonings.

But we do not need to mention their details and explanations. If it is in the meaning of being that is necessary, pure and limitless, you will indeed realize that such a being should necessarily be unique and not multiple. In explanation of the matter it can be said that existing beings are not other than of two kinds: either they are limited or unlimited and absolute.

Limited beings are those whose existence is having a limit and they do not possess the being and perfections of others and they can be negated from it. For example: the existence of man is limited because he is a man and that is why other things like plants and lifeless things are placed with him and they can be negated from him. It can be said: Man is not plant and lifeless matter and they are also not human.

Since such beings do not possess existence in the position of their own being, they are needful and they have to take their existence from others. In such limited beings multiplicity, imagination and possibility of occurrence is present. As it is said (in plural form): Human beings, animals, plants and lifeless matters.

The second type is unlimited beings: Since such beings do not have limits and quantities; on the contrary they are absolute, pure and unlimited. Since they are unlimited and do not have any defect, they possess all the perfections and are needless from every aspect and free of need in their being. In this supposition, the existence of the greater and more free of need is not there that it should be needed.

In such a being actually, there is no imagination of multiplicity. In front of a being that is unlimited, how can we imagine another being who is unlimited and which should be its partner in creating and controlling the universe? Because if the second supposed being also possesses all the perfections of the being and is a part of its being, and if it lacks some of the perfections of the rst being, he would be one and the same.

And if he lacks some perfection he would be limited and needful and such a being cannot be considered as a partner of God. This leads us to conclude that all phenomena of the world are limited and needful and are related to the Almighty Allah and we only have a single unique and pure being and He is one and has no partner.

Oneness in Attributes

Oneness in attributes means that the qualities of the Almighty Allah are His very being and not additional to His being. A few points can be mentioned to explain it:

1) Existing beings possess an existence and qualities; for example you see a white paper and say: This is a white paper. In this example, 'paper'

is the being and 'white' is the quality. Paper can be white and it cannot be white. Whiteness is incidental to the paper and it does not have a separate existence.

Whiteness is other than the paper and that is why it is possible for it not to be white.

Another example: Let us consider a knowing man. Here we have a knowing man and knowledge. Man is a being and knowledge is his attribute. Knowledge is not in the position of the being of man; on the contrary it is an incidental matter. If knowledge had been in the being of man, he would not have required acquiring it. Thus knowledge is neither the very being of man nor a part of his being.

2) Previously you read that the Almighty Allah possesses all the attributes of perfection. Since He is an unlimited being, it is necessary for Him to have all perfections. And if not, He would be decient, limited, needful and an effect. You also learnt about the qualities of perfection like knowledge, power, life, hearing and sight.

Now the question arises that of what type the qualities of Almighty Allah are? Are they like qualities of other people which are incidental and additional to their beings? Can the divine being of Almighty Allah be ever bereft of knowledge, hearing and seeing and are these qualities incidental to His being, as in the case of human beings? Or that the qualities of Almighty Allah are of some other kind? If you ponder on the above discussion, you would easily get the reply to this query?

In order to explain this we should say: The Almighty Allah is a being in such a way that His existence is unlimited, absolute, and pure and has no end. Positive attributes of such a being cannot be denied. And if not, He would be limited, decient and needful. Therefore knowledge, power and life and other positive attributes are the very being of Almighty Allah, and not incidental and additional to His being. That is why He is always in possession of the qualities and He does not need to acquire them.

The Almighty Allah is an unlimited being, and is knowledge, power and life itself. Since His being is Necessary Being (Wajibul Wujud), His knowledge, life and power would also be necessary and free of need of cause and unlimited; although He is only a single being and not more; but He is such an unlimited being that different meanings can be separated from Him.

With regard to Almighty Allah it is not that we should have a described being and the attributes be separate from Him; on the contrary, His divine being and positive attributes are in fact each other and He is one unlimited and absolute being.

In Nahjul Balagha, Ali Ibn Abi Talib (a.s.) has mentioned this critical matter and said:

"Perfection of sincerity is to deny Him attributes, because every attribute is a proof that it is different from that to which it is attributed and everything to which something is attributed is different from the attribute. Thus whoever attaches attributes to Allah recognizes His like, and who recognizes His like regards Him two; and who regards Him two recognizes parts for Him; and who recognizes parts for Him mistook Him; and who mistook Him pointed at Him; and who pointed at Him admitted limitations for Him; and who admitted limitations for Him numbered Him."[9]

Oneness in Creation

Creation is in the meaning of origination. Oneness in creation implies that Almighty Allah, since He is one in His being and does not have any partner, in creation also He is one and there is no creator other than Him. Previously we mentioned that beings are of two types: one is such that its being is its very existence and has no need of anyone or anything

---

[9] Nahjul Balagha, Sermon 1.

else. Secondly there are beings, which in the position of existence do not have independent existence and they need other beings to bring them into existence; and that is unique being of the Lord of the worlds.

That is why all phenomena of the world need Almighty Allah for their existence and they have no other who has given them existence, as the possible phenomenon since originally are needful of the holy being of Almighty Allah and in survival, continuity of being, and in their actions and effects are also related to and needful of this needless being. If they are not independent existence they also do not have independence in action and effects.

It is God who has brought them into existence and not made their beings null and void. That is why whatever is there, is from Almighty Allah and it does not have any creator and originator other than Him. This is the meaning of oneness in creation.

There is no power and strength except that of Allah, the High and the Mighty. Although phenomena of the world have effects; for example the Sun possesses light and heat, it helps in the growth of plants and plants in turn prepare food for animals and human beings. And hundreds and thousands of other effect like we see in Nature in this world; such effects cannot be denied, but they are not creators and originators. On the contrary in effect of natural actions or reaction the effects that are bestowed to them become obvious.

The creator of the universe is one who has given existence to natural beings and has bestowed effects and specialties to them. Scientists have made amazing new inventions through experiments and research, but with a little attention it can be concluded that they have not brought them into existence; on the contrary their most important achievement is the exposition of secrets hidden in material natures, which the creator of the world has placed in their beings. We do not negate the causality and effects and effectuality of the material world. On the contrary we also do not negate the independence of their effects. From these statements we can conclude that since the Almighty Allah is one in His being, He is also one in His creation and that He has no partners.

We can conclude from the Holy Quran that the polytheists of the Arabian Peninsula also confessed to oneness in creation.

The Quran says:

> *"And if you ask them, Who created the heavens and the earth and made the sun and the moon subservient, they will certainly say, Allah. Whence are they then turned away?" (29:61)*

And He says:

> *"And if you ask them Who is it that sends down water from the clouds, then gives life to the earth with it after its death, they will certainly say, Allah." (29:63)*

And He says:

> *"Is there doubt about Allah, the Maker of the heavens and the earth?" (14:10)*

And He says:

> *"Say: Allah is the Creator of all things, and He is the One, the Supreme." (13:16)*

And He says:

> *"He is Allah the Creator, the Maker, the Fashioner; His are the most excellent names..." (59:24)*

It can be concluded from such verses that the polytheists of the Arabian Peninsula and the ones addressed in the Quran knew that creation was from Almighty Allah and they were not polytheists in this matter. But it cannot be concluded from these verses that the polytheists of all areas of the world also have same belief and that they accept oneness of god in creation; as in the case of Zoroastrians; who believe that all good is created by Yazdan and all evil is created by Ahriman. However we would refute this belief in the discussion of monotheism through logical reasoning.

Oneness in Lordship and Will

We mentioned previously that since Almighty Allah is a unique and single being; He also is one in creation and has no partner in it. Now we shall prove that He is also one in Lordship and control of universe. First we should dene lordship and will and after that we should set out to reason out from them.

Lord in dictionary means one having something in His control so that He may reform its condition. Will is also in the same meaning: for example a piece of land is given in charge of a person in order that he may perform all necessary acts with regard to it. The gardener is identied as the lord and manager of the agricultural plot. The gardener is not the creator of the plot; on the contrary he is the lord and caretaker. Or for example if a person is given the power of creation and administrative matters are left at his discretion, he would also be called as the lord and controller. Or a man who is entrusted with the matter concerning quadrupeds; he is also considered as their lord and administrator.

Now the question arises that who is in control of the universe? Is it under the control of God, who has created it without any partner? Or He has handed over the charge of all or some of the phenomena to someone or something else? And this same matter is the topic of our discussion. From Quran and history it can be concluded that although the polytheists of the Arabian Peninsula accepted the oneness of god in creation, they did not ascribe to belief in the oneness of god in controlling and administering the world; on the contrary they considered other persons and things to be His associates in this regard.

Polytheists of the Arabian Peninsula, like polytheists of all countries of the world, believed that the Lord creator of the world (greater being) has entrusted the management of the world to invisible powers like angels, jinn, god of men, god of animals, god of seas and deserts, god of plants, god of human reproduction, holy spirits, evil spirits; so that they may control the world of nature independently and because of this belief, whenever they were confronted by dangers, calamities and to solve difculties and fulllment of needs they take refuge in a power related to the unseen; and to attract his attention perform offerings and rituals.

And as they were only 'imaginary' unseen powers, they shaped their images in wood, stone and metal and named them as idols and during worship focused their attention on them and humbled themselves before them while in fact their aim was to focus attention on unseen powers and different deities.

But the Holy Quran considers polytheism in lordship and will an invalid belief and also regards lordship as a special attribute of Almighty Allah. There are numerous verses in the Holy Quran which mention this point:

> *"Allah is He Who raised the heavens without any pillars that you see, and He is rm in power and He made the sun and the moon subservient (to you); each one pursues its course to an appointed time; He regulates the affair, making clear the signs that you may be certain of meeting your Lord." (13:2)*

And it says:

> "Surely your Lord is Allah, Who created the heavens and the earth in six periods, and He is rm in power, regulating the affair, there is no intercessor except after His permission; this is Allah, your Lord, therefore serve Him; will you not then mind?" (10:3)

Occupying the seat of authority and command (Arsh) is a simile for complete authority on the entire world to administer and ruling which is this same destiny and lordship. That is why lordship and divine will are also qualities only of Almighty Allah and the holy being of Allah from this aspect is also unique; and effect of causes and other cause will be there with His existential permission.

As mentioned in other verses also:

> "Nay! your Lord is the Lord of the heavens and the earth, Who brought them into existence..." (21:56)

And He says:

> "Say: What! shall I seek a Lord other than Allah? And He is the Lord of all things..." (6:164)

And He says:

> "All praise is due to Allah, the Lord of the Worlds." (1:2)

Therefore as the Almighty Allah is single in His being and creation and previously you have learnt about the argumentations of the same, in lordship and administering of the world also He is alone, without any partners. He controls the world and does not leave matters related to the whole world to anyone or anything else. Philosophical reasoning means the same that was mentioned in the oneness in creation.

There we mentioned that the possible phenomena of the world in His being and actions are needful of a being as His existence is free of need of others and such a being is not except the being of the Almighty Allah. It was also mentioned there that the worldly phenomena (visible and invisible) since they are dependent on a higher being for their existence, in their actions and effects also they are in need of that self-sufcient being and are fully dependent on it. We don't have a permanent and needless being among the worldly phenomena that lordship and control of the world can be entrusted to it.

And if we see causality and effectiveness in the phenomena of the world, we should consider them to be His direct actions and imagine that the control of the world is entrusted to it. On the contrary as mentioned in Quran, mediums and causes act through the permission of Allah. Although angels are mediums of divine favors and possess effects, but their inuence is not independent. In the same way, material causes have effect in the being of causality and not that they are independent; on the contrary they themselves and their effects are needful and dependent on Almighty Allah.

Oneness in Worship

Oneness in worship means monotheism and restricting worship only to the holy being of Almighty Allah. Oneness in worship was the most important call of the prophets. Quran says:

> *"And certainly We raised in every nation an apostle saying: Serve Allah and shun the Shaitan." (16:36)*

And He says:

"And We did not send before you any apostle but We revealed to him that there is no god but Me, therefore serve Me." (21:25)

Worship means servitude and obeisance and a special humility in front of the deity with the condition that the worship act should arise from belief in divinity, lordship, will and creatibility of the deity. Since divinity, lordship, will and creatibility are reserved only for the holy being of Almighty Allah worship and servitude should also be reserved for Him and no other being is eligible for this position and this is the meaning of oneness in worship.

As opposed to oneness in worship, we have polytheism in worship. It can be concluded from the Holy Quran that some people worship beings other than Allah, like: angels, unseen powers, sun and moon and some stars; they pay homage to them and make offerings and sacrices to them. Their worship arises from belief that those deities have lordship and control of the universe and they can guarantee the fulllment of their needs effectively and directly. They perform worships, offerings and sacrices to be noticed by them. And if they paid homage before the idols of stone, woods and metals, it was because they considered them to be an expression of those hidden beings and through invalid conjectures considered their worship to be a medium of divine proximity, while they cannot do anything. Quran has ridiculed the polytheists for this worship and says: Worship Allah as He is the doer of the world. The Holy Quran says:

"Say: Do you serve besides Allah that which does not control for you any harm, or any prot?" (5:76)

And says:

> *"You only worship idols besides Allah and you create a lie; surely they whom you serve besides Allah do not control for you any sustenance..." (29:17)*

And says:

> *"And surely Allah is my Lord and your Lord, therefore serve Him; this is the right path." (19:36)*

And said:

> *"O men! serve your Lord Who created you and those before you so that you may guard (against evil)." (2:21)*

And said:

> *"Certainly We sent Nuh to his people, so he said: O my people! serve Allah, you have no god other than Him..." (7:59)*

And said:

> *"And they serve beside Allah what can neither harm them nor prot them, and they say: These are our intercessors with Allah." (10:18)*

And said:

> *"...they were enjoined that they should serve one God only." (9:31)*

And said:

> *"Say: I am only commanded that I should serve Allah and not associate anything with Him..." (13:36)*

As you must have noted, the Holy Quran negates the lordship, divinity and creation of false deities and their worship; and declares it to be a wrongful and useless act and considers worship to be reserved only for the Almighty Allah as lordship and control of the universe is reserved for Him alone. In the previous lessons we have learnt through philosophical reasonings and there is no need to repeat it again.

As mentioned in the history of worship (religion), every humility, even the goal of humility cannot be taken to be an implication of worship, on the contrary humility in worship is that it should have come from belief in divinity, creation and lordship of the deity. And that is why the prostration of angels before His Eminence, Adam; since Almighty Allah had ordered it, it was not polytheism. Quran says:

> *"And when We said to the angels: Make obeisance to Adam; they made obeisance, but Iblis (did it not). He said: Shall I make obeisance to him whom Thou hast created of dust?" (17:61)*

It is known that prostration before His Eminence, Adam (a.s.) was not worship and polytheism, otherwise Almighty Allah would never have ordered it. And in the same way, the prostration of Prophet Yusuf and his brothers in front of their parents was not worship and polytheism as mentioned in Quran that Prophet Yusuf (a.s.) seated his parents on the throne and fell down in prostration to them along with his brothers.

> *"And he raised his parents upon the throne and they fell*

down in prostration before him." (12:100)

It is learnt that the prostration of angels for Adam (a.s.) and the prostration of Prophet Yusuf (a.s.) and his brothers for Prophet Yaqub (a.s.) was not worship and polytheism. Because angels, Prophet Yusuf (a.s.) and his brothers did not prostrate before Adam (a.s.) and Yaqub (a.s.) due to belief in their divinity, creation and lordship. On the contrary it was on account of respect and honor.

Kissing the Black Stone and touching it and circling the Kaaba in the holy religion of Islam is considered as worship act and it is ordered to perform it. In spite of the fact that the goal of humility is Kaaba, it is not considered as polytheism. Therefore the Ziyarat of the holy tomb of the Holy Prophet of Islam and kissing of the sarcophagus and supplication near it also will not be considered as implied polytheism.

And in the same way, visiting the tombs of the Holy Imams (a.s.) and kissing their graves and seeking the mediation of those puried souls with Almighty Allah and praying and seeking their intercession are also not considered polytheism.

Because all visitors know that the Holy Prophet (S) and Holy Imams (a.s.) were servants of Almighty Allah and needful of Him. Their honor and respect is not due to belief in their divinity, creation and lordship. Respect of those holy tombs is only due to the fact that they are related to the holy souls of the Holy Prophet (S) and his chosen descendants and in traditions Almighty Allah has ordered paying respect to them, to keep their memory alive and express our loyalty to those chosen ones.

Mediation through these holy souls, which is proved beyond doubt in Islamic law, is in fact obedience of the laws of Shariah and a medium of gaining proximity to Almighty Allah. You take advantage of natural causes in the matters of life and it is not polytheism, seeking mediation of holy souls of divine saints can also be from unnatural causes. But in any case neither natural cause have independence in their effects, nor unnatural cause; and they cannot be considered as polytheism.

Divine Justice

Divine Justice is a positive attribute and one of actions; implying that all acts of God are performed in accordance with justice and His holy being is pure of injustice. Divine justice is an Islamic belief and it is ascribed to by all Muslims in general, although there is difference of opinion in its interpretation between scholastic theologians and they are divided into two groups: Mutazali and Ashari or Adliya and Ghair Adliya.

In the Holy Quran, the quality of justice is proved for Almighty Allah and injustice is negated about Him. For example:

It is said in Quran:

> *"Allah bears witness that there is no god but He, and (so do) the angels and those possessed of knowledge, maintaining His creation with justice; there is no god but He, the Mighty, the Wise." (3:18)*

And He says:

> *"And the word of your Lord has been accomplished truly and*

justly; there is none who can change His words, and He is the Hearing, the Knowing." (6:115)

And says:

"Surely Allah does not do injustice to the weight of an atom, and if it is a good deed He multiplies it and gives from Himself a great reward." (4:40)

There is no doubt in the goodness of justice and evil of injustice. Everyone likes justice and praises one who is just; they consider injustice as evil and condemn the unjust. Justice has many denitions, but this is not the time to mention them or to do any research on this topic.

The best denition is that which is derived from the words of Nahjul Balagha: Imam Ali (a.s.) has mentioned justice to be superior to generosity and he says:

Justice is placing everything in its appropriate place.[10]

Justice implies fulllment of the rights of all those who have a right.

Every person, according to his creation, has some special rights and others are duty-bound to honor them; like the right to work and possession of the fruits of their labor, right of security and freedom, life and right of education, right to marry and reproduce and tens of other rights; just as one who respects the right of others in his society and he does not trespass on them. We can use two reasonings to prove justice of Allah and to negate that He is unjust:

---

[10] Compilation of Nahjul Balagha, Pg. 131.

The First Proof Is Quran

The Almighty Allah in numerous verses of Quran has ordered justice and equity and He has prohibited injustice and cruelty.

We present three verses by way of example:

> **"Surely Allah enjoins the doing of justice and the doing of good (to others)..." (16:90)**

> **"O you who believe! be maintainers of justice, bearers of witness of Allah's sake..." (4:135)**

> **"And do not think Allah to be heedless of what the unjust do; He only respites them to a day on which the eyes shall be xedly open." (14:42)**

The God, who has commanded justice and equity to people, and warned them against injustice and cruelty; how is it possible that He should Himself be unjust to His creatures.

The Second Is Logical Proof

One who does not observe the rights of others and oppresses them, is not in other than some conditions: either he does not perceive the evil of injustice or he is needful of that which he takes from the oppressed; or usurps the fruits of their labor in order to remove his deciency or he does not have the power of fullling their rights. Or he is miserly and he observes miserliness in fullling the rights of others or commits injustice by way of revenge or a vain past time.

But none of these possibilities exist with regard to Almighty Allah, because you have seen before He is all-knowing and wise and He performs all His actions under the dictates of His knowledge and wisdom, and ignorance is not found in His being. He is in possession of all perfections and is not decient in any of them.

He is the owner of all perfections and does not have any defect so that He should need to oppress others in order to make up for His deciency. He is benecent and generous and His own possessions are not reduced in bestowing them to others so that He should be miserly in it. He is absolute power and

He does not weaken by giving power to others.

Therefore since injustice is an evil act whose evil is perceived by all sensible beings, Almighty Allah is also pure of injustice. He bestows perfection to every existing being, including man, according to its capacity and capability and He does not trespass any of their rights.

Justice in Creation

Justice in creation is in the meaning that consideration must be observed with regard to capacities in creation of existing beings of the world and from the side of Almighty Allah there is no hindrance of grace and unlawful discrimination is exercised and in explanation of this statement, it is necessary to understand the following points:

First point: Phenomena of the world of existence can be divided into two kinds: abstract world and material world.

1. Abstract world: Abstractions are existing beings, which do not have movement and growth; they are from the beginning as they should be and in terminology they have absolute functions and are not material and physical; they are not visible; they neither deteriorate nor die. They are mediums of divine favors and they have no disobedience or opposition.

These invisible beings in the terminology of religion are introduced as angels, armies of God, destiny, distributor, throne, chair, tablet and pen. From such denitions it can be concluded that between the creator of the world and the phenomenon of the existing world there are connections which are invisible. In other words, the system of creation has come into being with a particular sequence and is being administered in this way. Angels are enforcers of divine commands and they never disobey or oppose God.

> *"...they do not disobey Allah in what He commands them, and do as they are commanded." (66:6)*

Also:

> *"And there is none of us but has an assigned place." (37:164)*

It is said that the positions of angels are divinely ordained and not by way of gaining eligibility for the same; such that each of them have a special existence and their responsibilities are derived from it. It should not remain unsaid that angels in their beings and actions do not have independence, on the contrary, they are mediums and not more than that and they are needful of and related to Almighty Allah who is needless, powerful, knowing and wise.

1. Material and physical world: Materiality as opposed to abstractness possesses a form and shape. They are changeable in essence and they have movement and growth. Material forms undergo changes, but the matter remains. When matter, under the effect of movement becomes capable to accept a new form it is bestowed that form; for example the apple tree; it possesses a matter and a form. Its form can be dened to be an apple tree, which grows and

gives fruits.

And its matter is dened as something, which has taken the shape of the apple tree. It means that the matter of the apple tree was having another form previously; for example it was an apple seed and it developed the capability to become a tree. After that the form of the tree was given to it. Then the tree became dried and its form changed and it turned into dust. But its matter is the same previous matter, but it does not have the signs of the apple tree. State of the matter, its form, change and transformation will continue in the same way.

The world of matter and materiality is very vast and human beings do not have perfect and correct knowledge about them. Our awareness is limited with the earth and limited number of earthly existing things like different kinds of plants, animals, minerals, water, air, light, heat and some knowledge of the sun and some stars; but we are mostly ignorant of the universe and galaxies and stars. We do not have perfect knowledge of the great universe, which is mostly unseen by us, although we have conducted extensive researches and still continue to do so; and the secrets unraveled so far are very less in comparison to the millions of secrets that still remain to be unraveled.

But that which can be said in brief is that all of them are phenomena of material beings which have evolved through ages under the effect of different natural factors to assume a new form and when new capabilities developed, they assumed a new form. We also do not have precise and complete awareness about the future of this movement and perpetual search. Glory be to Allah, the greatest.

Second point – Law of general causality: Previously we learnt the meaning of cause and effect. Effect is the phenomenon, which does not exist in its own being. Its existence and non-existence is same and it is in this aspect that it is needful of a cause. Cause is something on which the effect depends. Between every cause and effect there is a relation of particular originality. Every effect is not created by every cause.

And every effect is not resultant of every cause. If the cause is a phenomenon, it is itself in need of a cause. And in the same way, its cause and the cause of its cause, and this continues till we come to a cause, which is not a phenomenon. That is a being free of need and self-sufcient in its existence and

that is the Almighty Allah who is a necessary being (Wajibul Wujud) and who is also called as the cause of all causes.

Therefore, the law of cause and effect is a complete and all-encompassing law, which controls the world of existence and which has endowed it a system. Almighty Allah has created the universe and He controls it through the system of cause and effect. The world is having discipline and it follows a xed law; it is administered by the command of God. It is mentioned in the Holy Quran that:

"Surely We have created everything according to a measure. And Our command is but one, as the twinkling of an eye." *(54:49-50)*

In this legal system, every phenomenon holds a particular position and does not infringe it. If it had been other than this, the whole system would have collapsed.

Now we shall explain divine justice in creation in detail: Divine justice in creation implies that the origin of the creation of man and the distinctive qualities of all just persons is according to their capability and eligibility and denying grace and improper prejudice has not been resorted to.

According to this explanation, man is an existing being of the natural world. Like plants, he responds to nutrition, he has growth and reproduction; like different animals he possesses perceptions and intentional movement. Therefore he can be considered as a kind of plant and animal. But he is in possession of an important excellence, which is not present in other plants and animals.

Man has intelligence and reason, which is not found in any of the animals. The cause of this excellence is his abstract and ethereal soul to which the humanity of man is related. In terminology he is called as the 'form of human genus'. Like other existing beings, man also possesses matter as well as a form.

Matter of man is that which was present in another form previously and now it has assumed the shape of man and has accepted the abstract ethereal soul. Every matter is not capable to accept the human soul. Matters that have accepted the form of plants or animals cannot directly accept the human soul and become humans. It is only the seed of man (sperm) that can accept the soul of man and become a human being; and that also after many amazing changes and growths.

The seed of man also was not a seed previously; on the contrary it was present in another form. It became a seed gradually and after undergoing changes. When the human sperm was placed in an appropriate place – that is in the womb of a mother – it mixed with the female egg and becomes capable of accepting the human soul and it is joined to it and it should be as such since Almighty Allah is not miserly.

But human beings also all are not same from the aspect of sense, memory, form, skin color, height and physical perfection or deciency; on the contrary they are different from each other. These differences are also effects of the specialties of the parents and their ancestors; kind of nutrition of the parents is effective during pregnancy and lactation; their environment, health or sickness of the father mother or grandparents. The sperm, which accepts the form of a special human being, is capable in this way and according to the system of cause and effect should be created like this.

Therefore every man in the system of cause and effect possesses a special position and according to special qualities, which his matter has bestowed has the eligibility of being and in the same way and without injustice and discrimination obtains the being and perfections of being. But if it is other than this, it should be that the universal law of cause and effect will be deranged and the original system will go awry and basically will not create existence.

Therefore justice in the creation of man and the world implies that phenomenon of the world, including human beings are according to the capability that they have developed eligibility of being and in the same quantum and in the same manner are given similar existence, perfections of being, and denying grace and improper prejudice has not been resorted to.

Divine Justice and Objections Against It

Divine Justice is an important Islamic topic, which is discussed everywhere in books of theology and philosophy. Philosophers and scholars of Islam believe in it and they defended it energetically; on the other hand some opponents have denied and refuted justice of Allah and have expressed doubts in this regard and still do it. They consider destructive earthquakes, damaging oods, children born disabled and diseased, differences between human beings, presence of carnivorous beasts and poisonous reptiles as signs of the absence of justice in creation and in this way they have also denied the root of the existence of the creator of the world and also created doubts in resurrection.

Therefore, in present conditions, need is felt for a plan to prove the matter of divine justice and replying to the doubts. Discussion of justice and replying to objections against it is one of the important points of philosophy and theology, which is studied in detail in books of philosophy and theology and proved as a fact. Regretfully all those objections cannot be studied fully in this brief writing, but in order to assure that none of the doubts remain unanswered, we shall mention their simple and brief replies. The most important objections and their replies can be divided into four groups:

First: Natural Calamities

Like destructive earthquakes, damaging oods, terrifying storms and other natural calamities are included in this group. It is said: Occurrence of these bitter happenings, which are mostly accompanied by great losses in terms of life and property; how can they be compatible with divine justice. Why He does not prevent such incidents? Why He has created the world in this way?

In brief, it can be said that such kinds of occurrences, like natural happenings are as a result of particular causes, on the other hand previously you have seen that Almighty Allah has created and He administers the world of nature and material phenomena through the system of cause and effect; and that He has arranged the world according to the system of cause and effect and not that He rst created the phenomena and after that He gave cause and effect to them; on the contrary cause and effect in their very essence are related to each other. Each of the causes and effects are placed in a particular position and negation of each of them would be construed as denial of the total system. For example, look at the stages of numbers: each of the numbers (1-2-3…and so on) holds a special position. Number ve cannot take the place of ten and vice versa. It is not possible to completely remove number ve from the serial of numbers. Its removal would imply removal of numeric system.

The system of creation is also like this. Every phenomenon holds a special position and is connected to its natural cause. It terminates at the cause of the causes; that is Almighty Allah as His being is free of need of others. All phenomena of the world of existence has come into existence through His intention and they are administered by the same; but not through different intentions; on the contrary through a widespread intention. Quran says:

"And Our command is but one, as the twinkling of an eye." **(54:50)**

Therefore earthquake is a natural phenomenon and according to the statement of experts, it has numerous benets with it and in the system of nature it is considered to be an important matter. They say: If there had been no earthquakes, there would have been no mountains. And if mountains had not been there, there had been no rain and snow; and if rain had not been there, plant, animal and human life would have not been possible.

Although sometimes, some earthquakes are accompanied by destruction of life and property, which are requisites of competition between natural phenomena it cannot be expected from Almighty Allah that He should personally intervene in case of destructive earthquakes and prevent them as preventing it would be only possible by negating its cause and it would necessitate the derangement of system of creation.

Preventing the damages of earthquakes is the function of human beings themselves. Almighty Allah has given sense and intelligence to man, so that through gaining knowledge and experience he may understand the causes and factors underlying the earthquakes; and through the reins of natures he may prevent the damages caused by them; or at least minimize them; that he should not inhabit areas prone to earthquakes and avoid constructions there; as some countries have taken profound steps in solving this problem.

Especially, the same thing can be said with regard to damaging oods: Floods are caused by heavy rains due to slope of surfaces of the earth and uidity of water. Therefore the owing of oods in special circumstances is a natural phenomenon as it is the effect of a particular cause. Falling of rain on highlands, sloping of land and owing of water is among the great divine bounties, which provide life to plants, animals and human beings.

And all of them are good in their own position; have you so far thought that if rain had not fallen on highlands or if the earth had not been sloping or if the nature of water had not been owing, how our life would have been? Although their necessary factor is such that in some instances there will be oods entailing loss of life and property and the responsibility of preventing these losses rests on sensible human beings. He must not build residential buildings in ood prone areas and that he must strengthen his constructions in accordance to the possibility of oods. If man falls short in this regard and suffers losses, it is due to his own shortcoming.

Second: Children born with physical defects

One of the instances that refute divine justice is the creation of children born with physical defects. Like children who at the time of birth are deaf, dumb, blind, paralyzed, disabled, insane or spastic. It is said: Existence of such deformed children who are compelled to lead a difcult life and their parents also have to suffer a great deal on account of them; how can it be compatible to divine justice? Why they do not possess perfect physical health like other children? And why they were created at all? Is it not injustice?

In reply to this doubt, it can be said: The defect of these children is either due to genetic mutation through the parents or can also be as a result of inappropriate diet of the parents, especially of the mother during pregnancy and lactation. Or as a result of toxic and harmful matters that it may come in contact with during fetal development in a dirty environment. Or it can be due to an injury received during its fetal stage.

In any case, the defect of the newborn is related to the defect of the matter that has accepted the form of human being. Almighty Allah has not given a defective existence to such children; on the contrary He created them but their capacity of accepting matter was not more than this. Special capacity and capability of the matter of each of them also would be the effect of the cause and its special causes.

Two questions arise at this point: Firstly, the God who is aware of the defect of this matter, why did He bring that defective human being into existence? Secondly, is the Almighty Allah not capable of bestowing a perfect and healthy matter to man?

In reply to the rst question, it can be said: As mentioned previously, the existence of material phenomena is related to a particular capability that develops in that matter. Every capability that develops in that matter is according to the form, which would be given to it. Matters which develop the capability to create the form of human beings would be given human forms. Human soul is good and perfection, it should be increased, nally it is that if this matter is having the capacity of physical maturity it will mature in the proper manner and if there was defect in it, it would be deprived of perfect maturity.

In reply to the second question, it can be said: As mentioned previously, Almighty Allah has created and manages the phenomena of existence through causes and effects and it is through this that the world is arranged. It cannot be expected from Almighty Allah to personally intervene in some circumstances, and that without natural causes He should assure the perfect development of a thing, which does not possess perfect matter. It would imply that Allah in some instances nullies the law of cause and effect causing disruption of the system of the world; and this is not acceptable. In other words, there is no doubt in the power of Almighty Allah but His power cannot be related to a logically impossible matter and the derangement of the system of cause and effect is from the logically impossible matters.

Therefore, defects which are seen in children are due to defective sperm and lack of capability of the sperm with which the soul of man was added. And those defects themselves also were effects of their special cause and were necessary factors of the material world and a product of competition of material beings and their prevention is not possible except through prevention of occurrence of their natural causes. Allah has bestowed man with intelligence and sense, so that he may discover through study and experience the causes of these defects and that he may use this knowledge in childbirth; on the contrary even at the time of selecting the spouse; and that he may observe all the rules of hygiene in his environment and nutrition during pregnancy and delivery and can prevent the birth of defective children to the maximum.

It is possible that someone might say: In case the parents and those responsible for making the environment healthy and general hygiene do not fulll their obligations and they brought a defective child into this word; but what is its fault that it is compelled to spend its life in extreme difculties? We reply: Although he is not responsible for this, Almighty Allah has also not made him responsible more than what he can bear. He is a man and every man is given spiritual perfection according to his capability and efforts. His patience and forbearance would also not remain unrewarded and in the world after death, he would be recompensed for them. His parents and other caretakers would also be rewarded well.

Third: Differences between Individuals

Another excuse for objecting to the justice of God is the difference of complexion, beauty and ugliness, intelligence and memory, physical powers and other types of such matters. It is said that all human beings have right to live, why are they created with such differences? Why all human beings are not given equal intelligence? What is the fault of ugly people that they are created so ugly? Are such differences not discrimination and injustice?

In reply, it can be said: These differences or causes of different capabilities were present in the eggs of the parents and which they inherited from their ancestors or it is the effect of the parts and environment of their life or it is the effect of type of nutrition of the parents, especially that of the mother during pregnancy. In any case, differences in human beings are due to differences in their natural capabilities. In other words, differences cannot be denied, but they should not be considered as improper prejudice; prejudice is justied only when two seeds which were same from the aspect of capability are given two kinds of perfection of existence; while the fact is that it is not so.

Fourth: Existence of Harmful Creatures

It is said that the existence of harmful creatures, like carnivorous beasts, poisonous reptiles, different harmful viruses and microbes which pose danger to the life and safety of human beings and some animals; how can they be compatible with divine justice? What is the benet of such harmful creatures? And why were they created at all?

In reply it can be said: Generosity and benecence of Almighty Allah demands that He must bestow existence to every matter, which develops in itself the capability to accept a soul in proportion of its capability. If it develops the ability to accept the soul of animals, it would be given the soul of wild and harmful beasts, the soul of animals will be added to it and if it develops the capacity of the existence of microbe, the same existence will be given to it.

Although such animals may be harmful to man, they are benecial and good to themselves. Although the scorpion is harmful for human beings, it is good and perfection for itself. Moreover, the existence of these animals is absolutely benecial although man has not yet discovered those benets. Our ignorance is not a proof of their uselessness.

Almighty Allah has given intelligence and sense to man so that he may gain benets from even poisonous animals and that he may prevent their harms. Man is able to even confront harmful viruses and microbes by observing hygiene and by using antibiotics; and he can neutralize them effectively. Therefore the existence of harmful animals cannot be considered as evil and absence of justice in creation.

Role of Justice in Prophethood

Justice is one of the qualities of the acts of God implying that all acts of God are based on justice and that He does not oppress anyone. This fundamental is not present only in the creation of existing beings, as was mentioned previously; on the contrary it is the basis of all the principles of faith like prophethood, Imamate and resurrection also. If someone has doubt in divine justice, he can also not prove the authenticity of prophethood, Imamate and resurrection. In the discussion of prophethood, divine justice is used as reasoning in four instances:

The First Instance

The rst instance is about the framing of the laws of the Shariah and duties of people and conveying them through the prophets, which is called as general prophethood. In this discussion it is said as follows:

1. In philosophy and theology, it is proved through reasoning that although man is a reality and not more than one; he has a few stages of existence; on one hand he is a physical and natural body possessing its effects. Since he is a body, he requires nutrition and has potential for growth. On the other hand he has an animal soul;

and possesses perception and movement. But the highest stage of his existence is the abstract ethereal soul with which his humanity is connected.

2. It is proved that although the material body of man is prone to dissolution and death, his human soul has no death and annihilation; on the contrary at the time of death, he is transferred from this world to the world of the hereafter so that in the everlasting world of the hereafter, he may be recompensed for his good and bad deeds.
3. Man in this world has two types of lives: One is a vegetative and animal life, which is related to his physical body. Another is the inner life, which is related to the soul and spirit of man.
4. The spiritual life of man is related to the kind of beliefs, morals and his good and bad deeds. If he was having correct beliefs in the world and possessed good morals; and that he walked on the straight path; his ethereal soul would be perfected and it will be given a happy and successful life after death. And if he had harbored invalid beliefs and had bad morals and behavior; and was deviated from the straight path of humanity; he would sink into the dark valleys of bestiality and would have a difcult and painful life in the world of the hereafter.

The Holy Quran has, in numerous verses, introduced religion and religious law as the straight path; Almighty Allah as the guide and the prophets as warner and givers of glad tidings. For example:

"Say: Surely, (as for) me, my Lord has guided me to the right path; (to) a most right religion..." (6:161)

"And We would certainly have guided them in the right path." (4:68)

"...and Allah guides whom He pleases to the right way." (24:46)

"Say: The East and the West belong only to Allah; He guides whom He likes to the right path." (2:142)

"Surely Allah is my Lord and your Lord, therefore serve Him; this is the right path." (3:51)

"And We have not sent you but as a giver of good news and as a warner." (25:56)

As you have seen, in these verses and tens of others like them, religion and religious law is described as the straight path and Almighty Allah is introduced as the guide. Guidance is in the meaning of showing the way and it cannot be imagined without the presence of a path. Religion is dened as a collection of correct principles of faith, morals and laws and rules of religion; and it is the same straight path. Which we ask from Allah again and again in prayers that He may guide us to it:

"Keep us on the right path." (1:6)

With attention to what is said above we conclude that: The God who has created man and bestowed perfections to him, and through the power of perfection has equipped him and opened the way of perfection for him and so that in treading this difcult path, he should be in need of guidance and help;

He did not at all leave him in ignorance and without any duties. To abandon needy human beings is considered as injustice and an evil deed and the holy being of the wise, knowing and self-sufcient God will be pure of it.

Although in the discussion of general prophethood, the law of grace has been employed, but as you saw, belief in divine justice is very important. If divine justice is not accepted in proving the need of prophethood, relying on the law of divine grace would alone not have sufced and it would not have been able to reply to all the doubts.

The Second Instance

The second instance is about the distinctive qualities of the prophets: In the discussion of prophethood, it was proved that prophets possess distinctive qualities and the most important of them are the following three:

One: Complete knowledge; like the knowledge of laws and rules of religion; valid beliefs, good morals, which are needed by human beings.'

Two: Infallibility; that is immunity from mistakes, forgetfulness and sins.

Three: Power to perform extraordinary feats in instances when it is necessary to prove the veracity of the claim of prophethood.

These three qualities are considered necessary in prophet. In proving their view they have generally resorted to the 'proof of grace'; with the explanation that divine grace demands that His prophets should have the three above mentioned virtues so that they be most suitable for the guidance of human beings.

But I think that in this matter also it is better to take the benet of divine justice with the mention that sending of prophets who are ignorant of all or some of laws and in whose propagation there is chance of mistake or that who does not have a miracle to prove his prophethood, which is not compatible according to justice of Allah; because religion becomes decient in guidance of people on the right path and the divine being of Almighty Allah is pure of this.

Third Instance: Allotting Of Duties

In scholastic theology, it is proved that religious laws and duties should be according to the strength and capabilities of the people; in this also especially it can be concluded from verses of Quran and traditions as well as through logical reasonings. For example the Holy Quran says:

> *"Allah does not impose upon any soul a duty but to the extent of its ability." (2:286)*

> *"Allah does not lay on any soul a burden except to the extent to which He has granted it." (65:7)*

> *"And strive hard in (the way of) Allah, (such) a striving as is due to Him; He has chosen you and has not laid upon you any hardship in religion..." (22:78)*

> *"Allah does not desire to put on you any difficulty, but He wishes to purify you..." (5:6)*

This point is also mentioned in traditions; for example:

The Messenger of Allah (S) said: "Harm and causing harm are not sanctioned by Islam. Islam increases the benefits of Muslim and does not cause any evil to him."[11]

The Holy Prophet (S) also said:

"The Almighty Allah has made lawful everything about which a person is distressed."[12]

From such verses and traditions an absolute law can be derived that Almighty Allah in framing laws and duties has taken into consideration the strength of people, and the duty imposed on us is not difficult and intolerable. Through this command, we can derive a general law with regard to acts, which are harmful and difficult as the Holy Imams (a.s.)

---

[11] Mizanul Hikmah, Vol. 2, Pg. 180.

[12] Biharul Anwar, Vol. 75, Pg. 413.

have clarified them.

We can see numerous examples of them in the traditions of Ahl al-Bayt (a.s.) and the verdicts of the Islamic jurisprudents.

For example: One of the most important Islamic laws is with regard to fasting during the month of Ramadan, which are highly emphasized. But one for whom it is difficult to fast, is exempted from it.

Like those who are indisposed and the fast is harmful for them; the expectant women who are near to their term and the fast may be harmful to them or the fetus; travelers on a journey sanctioned by religion and aged persons for whom it is difficult to fast; all of them are allowed exemptions in keeping the fasts of Ramadan; although after Ramadan, in case their excuse does not exist anymore, they must make up for the lapsed fasts by keeping them now except for aged persons who are not bound to make up for lapsed fasts. Same order applies to other laws and religious duties.

Most of these excepted orders are mentioned in traditions in circumstances that there should not be a particular textual order about them and in case no such text exists, a general law can be derived with regard to acts which are impossible or beyond human capacity.

To prove this principle in addition to verses of Quran and traditions, we can also employ the 'rule of kindness'; with the explanation that:

Divine justice on people demands that the Divine law should not impose extremely difficult duties or expect them to perform deeds, which are beyond their capacity.

Apart from these, one can also make use of the principle of divine justice; with the explanation that imposition of duties, which are beyond human capacity and harmful is also an evil act and the holy being of Almighty Allah is pure from such acts.

It is said that in Islamic Shariah also there are some laws, which in the beginning seem to be absolute and difficult; like the obligatory nature of holy war and defense, which in addition to being difficult also sometimes ends in injuries and martyrdom of the fighters. But we should note the important point that Jihad is a logical matter and it is considered as a need of the social life of man.

This order is not restricted to Islam, on the contrary all heavenly religions, communities and sects in circumstances in which their beliefs, ideals, territories and their own community is surrounded by enemies, they know that their duty is to make efforts to defend it. Not only do they consider this difficult act to be a duty, which they cannot bear and a hardship, on the contrary they take precedence in loyalty and sacrifice. They consider their dead as martyrs and honor their memory. In Islam also it is in the same way; in verses of Quran and traditions sacrifice and loyalty in the way of Allah is praised and exalted and a high position is accorded for martyrs.

Fourth Instance: Justice of God in the World After Death

Divine Messengers throughout the period of history have always spoken of resurrection and the day of recompense. From the statement of Almighty Allah to the believers and pious He has promised Paradise and bounties of Paradise and in this way encouraged belief and good deeds. And to the infidels He has promised Hell and chastisement of the Hereafter. The basis of the call of the prophets was as such and through this the believers and righteous are given hope and the infidels and unjust are warned.

Now the question arises that whether Almighty Allah in the world of the hereafter would really fulfill His promise or that it is possible from Him not to fulfill His promise; or in contrast He would send the believers and the righteous to Hell and send the infidels and unjust ones to Paradise? Believer in divine justice say: Almighty Allah would definitely honor His promise since breaking of the promise is an evil deed and evil acts cannot be committed by Almighty Allah.

The same point is explained in numerous verses of Quran:

> *"And We will set up a just balance on the day of resurrection, so no soul shall be dealt with unjustly in the least..." (21:47)*

> *"So this day no soul shall be dealt with unjustly in the least; and you shall not be rewarded aught but that which you did." (36:54)*

> *"Allah does not impose upon any soul a duty but to the extent of its ability; for it is (the benefit of) what it has earned and upon it (the evil of) what it has wrought." (2:286)*

> *"And guard yourselves against a day in which you shall be returned to Allah; then every soul shall be paid back in full what it has earned, and they shall not be dealt with unjustly." (2:281)*

Here we consider it necessary to mention some important and subtle points:

It is concluded from traditions and verses that the reward and punishment of the hereafter is not a supposed and stipulated; on the contrary it is factual and conclusive and in the form of the good or bad morals that man had in the world. Paradise and bounties of Paradise are the unseen aspect of good morals and character of man and his attitude in the world, which would be exposed in the world of the hereafter. Hell and chastisement of the hereafter is also as such.

In the Holy Quran, it is said:

> *"On the day that every soul shall find present what it has done of good and what it has done of evil, it shall wish that between it and that (evil) there were a long duration of time; and Allah makes you to be cautious of (retribution from)*

Himself; and Allah is Compassionate to the servants." *(3:30)*

Therefore good or bad morals and good and bad character that man has in this world and which became the essence of man, would remain with him until Judgment Day and he would be resurrected along with it. Paradise and bounties of Paradise would be prepared from good morals and character and Hell and the different chastisements of the hereafter would be brought into existence through evil behaviors and despised morals.

Effect of Faith on Morals and Good Behavior

Knowing God, prophethood and resurrection are not imaginative and ineffective matters; on the contrary it is faith in the responsibility of creation and with action, and they are interdependent of each other.

Faith is like the root of a tree and good deeds are like branches, leaves and fruits of that tree. Faith and belief of conscience cannot be without the effects of deeds. On the contrary they are denitely followed by effects and necessities.

Through the medium of deeds, people can scale the stages of faith. As much strong the faith is; as much will be the effects owing from it. As less are deeds, the faith would also be as weak. One who expresses faith and religiosity, but the effects of faith is not visible in his deeds; or that he is faithless in his inward being and he makes a show of faith to deceive others or that he is having a very weak faith and he cannot put it into practice.

Faith is the source of deeds, fulllment of the vow of creation and religious duties. Faith impels man to submit before divine commands in all dimensions of life and to follow the programs and guidance of prophets. In numerous traditions, faith is explained in this way. For example Imam Ali (a.s.) says:

"I asked the Messenger of Allah (S): What is faith? He replied: Testimony by the heart, acceptance by the tongue and action by the physical organs and limbs."[13]

If faith has really permeated in the heart of man, its effect would be denitely seen in his words and deeds.

The believer in his whole being has accepted Almighty Allah and has faith in His existence. He considers himself answerable before Him and submits before Him and commands of prophets. He has accepted the reality that man and the world are not aimless and in vain and man has not come into existence to end in annihilation.

On the contrary, he has come for the perfection of his soul and to be transferred to the world of the hereafter and to continue his life in that world. He knows that every man is responsible for his own deeds and he would have to account each of his acts in this world. He would in any case have to face the consequences of his deeds. A believer has faith that death is not the end of life; on the contrary it is transfer from the temporal world to the world of effulgence and joy and an everlasting life in the hereafter.

How can a believer who has such faith be careless and ignorant of good morals, acts and words? Such a belief transforms the life of man in all dimensions and it turns his attention only towards one direction: seeking the pleasure of Allah through following the commands of prophets. Belief lies under the foundation of deeds and affects man in three ways:

---

[13] Biharul Anwar, Vol. 69, Pg. 68.

Morals

A believer has faith in spiritual life and he knows that he can construct and nurture his future personality in this world and that he would be raised with the same on Judgment Day.

If he is righteous, he would be good and successful in the future and if he is evil, he would have a dark and unfortunate future and that is why he always makes efforts to reform his self and purify his being from all sorts of impurities and strives to develop perfect traits of character. He also tries to strengthen his human and ethereal personality and to control his selsh and animal desires.

Worship

Since believer has faith in Allah and considers Him as the sole creator and controller of the universe, he submits before His greatness and unlimited power and worships only Him. He assures himself by Allah and remains inclined to Him. He also presents his requests to Him alone and is always seeking His refuge. He begs for His eternal power and through worship and remembrance of Allah, tries to perfect and nurture his self and seeks His proximity.

Social Responsibilities

A believer considers the political and social system as the best medium of success in his world and

hereafter and regards himself bound to fulll the duties imposed on him to perfection. When confronted by injustice and oppression, he strives most in establishment of social justice. The believer man regards himself to be connected to the great and unique community of Islam.

He considers greatness and well-being of the community as his personal success and well-being and he takes its weakness and degradation as his personal weakness and degradation. In his view, the members of the Islamic Ummah are parts of his physical body. He is always desirous to impart comfort to them and to maintain their health and also feels their pain and discomfort.

What he desires for himself, the same he desires for other Muslims. What he dislikes for himself, the same he dislikes for others also. As much as he is thoughtful of his personal comfort and prosperity, as much he tries for the well-being and comfort for others. Like he feels responsible for his own well-being and that of his family members in the same way he feels responsible for the well-being of the united community of Islam and Muslims as social responsibilities also originate from faith and shape an important aspect of Islam. A faith, which sends man to retirement and makes him indifferent to the future of society, is not true faith. The Messenger of Allah (S) said:

"One who does not arrange the affairs of Muslims is not a Muslim. And one who hears the entreaty of a Muslim and does not respond to it, is not a Muslim."[14]

Life of the prophets and important religious personalities is also the best testimony. They spent their nights in worship and in the battlefield were as brave as lions. They did not sit in recluse away from the problems of the world engrossed in worship and supplication; on the contrary they were also present in the forefront in the social sphere and public life.

And in confronting injustice, oppression and deprivation, they tried their very best; and strived to establish social justice. And in fulfilling these great responsibilities they did not inch in any way. They fought the unjust and tyrants and did not in any way fear hardships and difculties.

Yes, the school of monotheism, school of morals, piety, school of

---

[14] Al-Kafi, Vol. 2, Pg. 164.

worship and inclination to Allah, school of Jihad and steadfastness and loyalty, confronting injustice and inequity, enjoining good and forbidding evil; all of them originate from right faith.

It is said that since faith is the source of good deeds; just as good deeds also plays an important role in strengthening and steadfastness of faith. As much as we refrain from sins and bad character and as much as we try to perform good deeds, as much the effulgence of faith would increase in our hearts.

Therefore after faith in Allah, resurrection and prophethood, we should act on the commands of Allah so that we may scale the lofty stages of faith. One who is content only with a notional belief and he does not put it into practice, and who follows the selsh desires would not only fail to achieve the nal aim of life but gradually, lose his faith as well. Knowledge and deeds for the human soul are having the same position of two such great things that not having any of them would prevent man from scaling the high points of God-worship and wayfaring in the path of Almighty.

www.ingramcontent.com/pod-product-compliance
Lightning Source LLC
LaVergne TN
LVHW092049060526
838201LV00047B/1307